THE END OF POLITICS

POLITICS

AND THE BIRTH OF iDEMOCRACY

DOUGLAS CARSWELL

Biteback Publishing

First published in Great Britain in 2012 by
Biteback Publishing Ltd
Westminster Tower
3 Albert Embankment
London SE1 7SP
Copyright © Douglas Carswell 2012

ISBN 978-1-84954-422-1

10 9 8 7 6 5 4 3 2

A CIP catalogue record for this book is available from the
British Library.

Set in Chronicle and Foundry Form Gridnik

Printed and bound in Great Britain by
CPI Group (UK) Ltd, Croydon CR0 4YY

To C and K

CONTENTS

ACKNOWLEDGEMENTS

I have been helped in writing this book by many conversations with various friends over the past few years. I am particularly grateful to Daniel Hannan MEP and Mark Reckless MP for allowing me to bounce ideas off them. Tim Evans and Steve Baker MP gave me useful advice on monetary policy. Philip Booth and Matt Ridley made a number of helpful suggestions.

I am grateful to John Hrabe for providing me with some insights into American politics.

For supplying me with prompt and accurate research, and helping me with different drafts, I am grateful to Victoria Nilsson, Vicky Barr and Helen Morrison in my office.

You can find further discussion about some of the topics raised in this book on my blog site, TalkCarswell.com, and by following me on Twitter @douglascarswell.

BIOGRAPHY

D ouglas Carswell is a prolific writer, blogger and commentator. After careers in both broadcasting and fund management, and losing to Tony Blair as the Conservative candidate for Sedgefield in the 2001 election, he was elected to Parliament in 2005. In 2009, Douglas was nominated a Briton of the Year for his campaign to bring change to Westminster and voted Parliamentarian of the Year by readers of *The Spectator*.

Douglas blogs each day at TalkCarswell.com and has written for the *Guardian, Financial Times, Sunday Times, Mail on Sunday, Telegraph* and *Spectator*, as well as appearing on the *Politics Show, Newsnight*, Sky and Radio 4's *Week in Westminster* and *Westminster Hour*. His self-published book *The Plan: 12 Months to Renew Britain* (2008) which he co-authored with Daniel Hannan has sold over 20,000 copies.

Born in 1971, Douglas lived in Uganda until his late teens. He retains a close interest in the country he used to call home. He read history at the University of East Anglia and King's College, London and now lives in London and Essex with his wife and young daughter.

INTRODUCTION:
THE WORSE, THE BETTER

The West is broke. In Britain, America and most of Europe, governments have spent so much that entire countries face bankruptcy.

In 2010, the American government spent $1,900 billion more than it collected in tax. A year later, the US government borrowed $100 billion *each month* just to pay the bills. For every $5 it spends, the US government is in effect putting $1 on a public credit card. With approximately $15 trillion (twelve zeros) already on the credit card, it adds up to a pretty big bill.

The average American earns almost $70,000 a year, meaning that the United States appears outwardly wealthy. But as Charles Dickens's character Mr Micawber understood, prosperity is the difference between what you have coming in and what you have going out.

Against that $70,000 annual income, every American is liable for $131,368 of public debt, plus a further $1,031,131 to pay for all those unfunded promises their government has made.

If you thought America was mired in debt, take a look at Britain and Europe.

Britain's total public and private debts are proportionately even bigger at more than five times her entire annual economic output. In Spain, France and Italy, total debt is between three and four times annual output.

Public debt in Greece is 132 per cent of output, Italy 111 per cent, France 90 per cent, Ireland 85 per cent, Germany 83 per cent, Britain 81 per cent and Spain 71 per cent.[1]

Rich Western nations now have such large public debts they are in danger of growing poor. Like a runaway credit card bill, once debts reach such levels, the interest payments on the debt begin to grow faster than they can be paid back.

Greece, Italy, Spain and Portugal have reached this stage – which is why, for the first time since the Second World War, private lenders have stopped lending to them. Other countries have had to step in to bail them out.

The US government debt interest bill already means that every US citizen faces the equivalent of $11,000 in interest payments alone each year. Total debt payment on all American debt will be $50,000 per family by 2015.

There comes a point when debt not only becomes unmanageable, but begins to sap prospects for future growth. We are at that point.

Faced with runaway debts, governments begin to confiscate ever more wealth to pay for bloated state bureaucracies. Higher public spending designed to produce missing growth brings forth only more debt. Cheap credit is sluiced towards overconsumption and bad risks, producing still more debt.

The result is both relative – and perhaps even absolute – economic decline.

In 1990, the West accounted for over 80 per cent

of global GDP. Today it accounts for less than 60 per cent. Within the next seven or eight years it is likely to account for less than half. Since 2004, economic output in China has increased by 126 per cent, in India by 90 and Brazil 37.[2] In the West, by contrast, just about the only things growing are debts and taxes.

A stagnant West has been maintaining her living standards by borrowing off the dynamic, productive non-Western world. Already living standards in America are lower today than they were a decade ago. In Britain, living standards have fallen for three successive years, as they have across much of Europe.

Within the space of a generation, the West has gone from a position of global economic pre-eminence to bailout beggar.

What went wrong? How did the West end up in such a mess?

The West is broke financially because Western democracy has failed politically.

Western democracy used to be shorthand for a system of limited government. Each in its own way, Western democracies kept authority accountable, the demands of the governing tolerable and the taxes they imposed on the governed bearable.

The West is in debt because Western democracy has not been alive to the task of keeping government small. It has failed to rein in officialdom, allowing limited government to give way to Leviathan.

Throughout the West, legislatures have been sidelined. Public policy is made with little reference to the public. Of course elections still happen. Parties and candidates still run for office. But as a process for deciding how we are governed, none of this much matters.

Elections no longer really decide what governments do. Unsurprisingly, fewer people bother to vote.

Socialist-leaning France has a very different kind of electorate, you might imagine, compared to proudly individualistic America. Perhaps. But while it is forty years since France last ran a budget surplus, it will be many years before America does so again.[3] Setting aside what voters vote for, it turns out that both France and the United States are as bust as one another, each brought low by big, bloated government.

Democrat or Republican, Gaullist or socialist, Conservative or Labour – regardless of who holds office, it seems that those who wield *'kratos'*, or power, in Paris or Washington, are no longer accountable to the *'demos'*, or people. And no longer reined in, Western government has grown – and kept on growing.

However Western electorates seem to vote, they all seem to be presided over by the same kind of technocratic, managerialist elite. In Europe or America, central bankers make monetary policy. Treasury officials make tax-and-spend decisions. Judges decide the rules for welfare. An international mandarinate sets trade rules.

Unanswerable to the public in whose name they formulate public policy, those with the *'kratos'* have proved susceptible to all kinds of passing intellectual fads. From the idea of European monetary union to the notion of federal subsidies for Fannie Mae, experts and officials have been able to reinforce public policy failures long after they might otherwise have changed course. The result has been an endless succession of catastrophic public policy choices. Without outward accountability, the West is extraordinarily badly governed.

Throughout the West, government has overreached itself, doing too much, at such expense – and doing it so badly – that the Western model is now in crisis.

This book is about that crisis, and what it now means for the West.

Is it all doom and gloom? We might have high debts and hopeless politicians, but are things really so bad?

I grew up listening to an endless succession of doom-mongers promising us catastrophes that never happened. First came dire warnings of global famine and overpopulation. Then it was demographic collapse and an obesity epidemic that was supposed to alarm us. In the 1970s, we were warned of a new ice age. Now it is prophecies of global warming. From Y2K to vaccine-resistant bugs, from bird flu to asteroid strikes, there has been no shortage of pessimists who turned out to be wrong.

Are the debt crisis and the bankruptcy of our political system really causes for despair?

Actually, no. Things might be bad, but they are going to start getting better.

The West's Big Government model might be bust. So Western governments will have to get a lot smaller.

It is not just maths and money. Technology – the digital revolution – means that the Big Government model has reached the end of the road.

Why, do you suppose, government in the West managed to get so big to start with?

Contrary to widespread myth, Western governments did not grow big because their 'demos' demanded it. Far from causing government to grow, as we shall see, democracy once reined it in.

Government started to grow big when those with the *'kratos'* – the powerful elite – learnt to subvert the democratic constraint.

How did they manage it? By concealing the costs of all that extra government from the *'demos'*.

Taxation, in the words of King Louis XIV's finance minister, Jean-Baptiste Colbert, is the art of 'plucking the goose to obtain the largest amount of feathers with the smallest amount of hissing'. In a democracy, if too many geese hiss too loudly, the government cannot pluck many feathers.

Western elites discovered how to pluck feathers from the geese without too much hissing using techniques that the former French finance minister could have only dreamed about.

The first method was through unequal taxation. So long as every goose had to have an equal number of feathers extracted, there would always be a danger of a flock of angry geese. Extract most of the feathers from a minority of the geese at any one time, however, and the hissing is confined to a few.

Thus was so-called 'progressive' income tax born almost a hundred years ago. The growth of Big Government soon followed.

The second technique Western elites began to use to extract feathers without us noticing was by manipulating the money. Impossible while currencies were linked to gold, over the past forty years Western governments have been able to deliberately debase the currency. A few percentage points each year on the Retail Price Index measure of inflation soon adds up. As we shall see, it amounts to a substantial transfer of wealth from private citizens to the public sector.

Increasingly Western governments are discovering that they cannot keep borrowing money in order to live beyond their tax base. They are about to discover that in the age of the internet the nature of their tax base is changing, too.

No longer will they be able to count on massed ranks of geese waiting to be plucked via the payroll as there once were. When so much is only a mouse-click away, it is no longer only the very rich geese that can take flight.

Taxes are going to have to become flatter, shared out proportionately across the electorate as a whole. And if the electorate as a whole begins to shoulder a more equal share of the costs of Big Government, all of a sudden it might not be quite so electorally appealing any more.

Nor, as we shall see, in the age of the internet, will governments keep on being able to manipulate the money.

Unequal taxation, excessive borrowing and monetary manipulation – the three pillars on which Big Government is built – are beginning to crumble.

The digital revolution will not only limit the ability of government to keep living beyond its means. It is starting to mean that the idea things should be organised by officialdom in the first place is on the wane.

How best to organise human social and economic affairs is one of the oldest political questions asked since civilisation began.

There has never been a shortage of different answers. 'According to the socialist blueprint', many used to say within living memory. 'According to Communist teachings', said others. Or Catholic teachings, thought others.

The blueprints might have varied, but attempts to

order human affairs according to such blueprints has been a constant theme throughout history.

Only relatively recently have a small number of people – until now very much on the margins of political debate in most Western countries – started to suggest that perhaps the best way of arranging human social and economic affairs is not to have any grand designs at all.

Instead of organising things according to a blueprint, perhaps things should be left to organise themselves. Rather than arrange human development in accordance with what one group of people think is best for the whole, let it happen organically and spontaneously.

The internet is itself a sprawling network of organic and spontaneous design. Each time you do a Google search, you are harnessing the wisdom and knowledge of millions. The web is not merely a collective endeavour without any central directing authority. It makes collective endeavours free from a directing authority possible on a size and scale that was previously impossible. The digital age is favourable to the idea of spontaneous and organic design. Collectivism without the state – the dream of every anarchist in history – begins to seem possible, practical and mainstream.

Growing up in the 1980s, the idea that everyone might one day have their own personalised radio station would have seemed absurd. How could you have enough listeners to make it worthwhile? The very idea would have implied vast uneconomic cost.

Yet today personalised radio stations are pretty much exactly what millions of people have when they listen to their iPod or manage their playlist on Spotify. The digital revolution has made what seemed unattainable and far-fetched thirty years ago common-place and unremarkable today.

Government today runs public services the way it used to run radio stations in Britain. Planners decide what you get the way radio DJs once decided what you could listen to. However much they might try to respond to individual requests, the one-size-fits-all nature of the medium means most people will not get exactly what they want, the way they would if they could select things for themselves.

Public services, like music playlists, will be increas-ingly managed by those who use them. Instead of a national school curriculum, why not have parents and teachers tailor a personalised curriculum for each child? Rather than a medical care package or home care support commissioned for your elderly relative by officials, why not design the assistance you know they really need?

Public administration need no longer be something done for the public by officialdom. Increasingly it could be done by the public for themselves. Even if we were still able to afford the Big Government model, technol-ogy means that we no longer need to have collective choices made through government.

Ten, or even five, years ago, what sort of news we listened to or read about was chosen for us all. A distant editor picked a selection of news items and put them into a half-hour broadcast or a newspaper for the rest of us.

You might have only been interested in the cricket scores or the celebrity gossip or the financial news. But, like me, you would have had to buy a whole newspaper or watch the whole news just to pick up the bit that interested you.

Today that is changing. Twitter allows us to each build our own personalised newsfeeds about the things that interest us. Rather like those ticker-tape feeds that keep traders informed about share prices in City dealing rooms, our Twitter account becomes our own personalised news feed – but one that is tailor-made for us. We select which media organisations, friends or interest groups to follow.

What was once chosen for us in aggregate we now select for ourselves as individuals. If how we consume news can be personalised, how we consume government and public services can be as well. No longer will we be handed government as subjects. We will commission the bits of government we want as individual citizens.

With fewer one-size-fits-all decisions foisted upon us, there will be less need for public officials to make one-size-fits-all choices at all. Public choices will be increasingly made by the people for themselves. More and more of the decisions that affect our lives will be made by us, rather than by elected representatives on our behalf.

Moribund democracy, which has failed to rein in government, is about to be replaced by a system of iDemocracy, which will allow us to deconstruct much of the state.

PART 1

THE END OF POLITICS

CHAPTER 1

GOVERNMENT KEEPS
GETTING BIGGER

What is the biggest purchase that you will ever make? The mortgage on your home? The half-dozen cars you might get through over the years? Fees for university or college? Holidays? A lifetime's worth of food and clothes?

No. By far the largest bill is the one you get for government.

For every $100 that the average American worker earns, $36 is spent on buying government – $29 directly in various payroll taxes[4] and $7 in various consumption taxes when your average American tries to spend the rest of his pay packet.[5] Indeed, he has to pay for the big-spend items, like the house, car, college or food, out of the $64 that remains.

In Britain, the average worker buys £46 of government for every £100 earned. In Japan, it is ¥33 of every ¥100 earned. In France and Germany, after spending €59 paying for government, the average worker has only €41 left to spend on themselves.[6]

HISTORICAL GROWTH

How different it once was.

In 1900, an English household typically spent 8.5 per cent of what they earned on government – a figure little changed since the days of the medieval tithe. In the United States and Europe, households spent between 5 and 15 per cent of earnings on government.

Ratios of general government expenditure, including transfers, to money GDP at market prices (per cent)

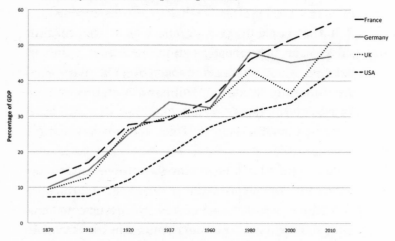

'From the founding of the Republic to 1929', wrote Milton Friedman of America, 'spending by government at all levels ... never exceeded 12 per cent of national income except in times of major wars. Federal spending typically amounted to 3 per cent or less.'[7]

'Since 1933', he continued, 'government spending has never been less than 20 per cent of national income and is now over 40 per cent.' After spiking sharply during the Second World War, there was a significant sustained increase in federal government spending between 1960 and 1980.

Perhaps even more significantly, in the thirty years since Friedman complained of the 'ten-fold' increase in government, there has been no let-up in the rate at which government has kept on growing.

Despite a brief lull in the late 1980s and early 1990s, the growth of government has accelerated. Since 2007, government spending in the US has increased from 34 to over 40 per cent of GDP.[8] In Britain and France, government now accounts for over half of national income.

In the couple of minutes since you started reading this chapter, the size of US national debt alone – the gap between what government spends and what government takes in taxation – will have increased by over $5 million. By the time that you finish it, it will have increased by $50 million.[9] Total public debt amongst advanced Western nations will have risen by almost $100 million.[10] It won't take long before it begins to add up to some serious money.

Across much of the Western world, government has now grown to a size that would have seemed unthinkable to mainstream politicians just a generation ago. To put it in perspective, many of those countries that spent the last century pursuing a free market approach now have bigger state sectors than those who followed Marx. Former Soviet Russia has a state sector smaller than the United States'. China's state sector is approximately half the size.

It is not simply that we spend ten times more of what we earn on government than our great-great-grandparents did. With a massive increase in our earnings, the total resources allocated to government have increased by a magnitude of thirty to forty times what they were. It is a far larger slice of a much bigger pie.

Should this surprise us? Isn't it obvious that as people get richer they want to buy more of something? And as they get richer they choose to buy more government.

Except it is not true. As a rule of thumb, the richer people get the *less* they tend to spend on those things they already have, and the more they spend on things they previously survived without. Indeed, it is because they are able to do this that they get richer.

Western living standards rose over the past century or so precisely because Western households were able to spend a smaller portion of their household income buying higher quality basics. This has left us free to spend the higher disposable income we have left over on all those things our great-grandparents somehow managed to do without – like entertainment, travel or frivolous iPad apps.

Today, Western households spend a lot less of their income buying much more.

Take the average American earner in 1900. He or she would have spent $76 out of every $100 earned to pay for basics like food, clothing and shelter.[11] Today, they spend a mere $37 on food, clothing and housing.

In England during the eighteenth and nineteenth centuries, the typical English worker spent between 80 and 90 per cent of what they earned on food, clothing and shelter. In 2005, the average British consumer spent a mere 40 per cent on such basics.

Not only do we spend less on such things, but the food, clothing and housing that we buy is generally speaking of far superior quality to that which was available, at greater cost, to our great-great-grandparents.

The average British household, for example, might today only spend a mere 17 per cent of what they earn on food,[12] but whether it allows them to eat out or gives them a well-stocked fridge, they eat vastly better than they would have done a century ago. So much so, in fact, that the average Brit is now four inches taller than their great, great grandparents.[13] Overnourishment – or rather obesity – is now a greater public health problem than malnourishment.

If more-for-less has been the rule for Western spending patterns, government has been the great exception. Throughout the past century, we have been buying not more government for less income, but more government for an ever greater slice of what we earn.

This is partly because government today provides us with so much more than before. In the 1890s, when an English household spent around a tenth of their income on government, they were paying the bill for the Royal Navy, the Army, maintaining law and order, and perhaps a little infrastructure here and there. And that was about it.

Today, when the average English household stumps up an estimated £656,000 tax bill over the course of their lifetime,[14] they are buying health care, education, social security, street lighting and pension protection, too. Things that government simply never provided before.

But that is only part of the story.

We might be handing over thirty to forty times more resources than our great-great-grandparents did to pay for more government. But that is not to say that we are getting thirty to forty times more public services than they did. It means we are getting thirty to forty times more officialdom – some of which might mean more services. More often than not, it does not mean more services.

Public service productivity data from the UK and almost every other Western country shows that £1 more spending results in a lot less than a £1 increase in public service provision. Why? Because when we pay all that tax, we are not just paying for the Royal Navy and the police, or even for more health care or education or social security.

We are also paying for a vast sprawling apparatus of government – for community outreach workers, transformation managers, cluster coordinators. And for endless projects run in the interests of those on the public payroll, which just occasionally might also mean more of actual services that you or I might actually want.

Unlike the government, those who supply us with say food or clothing face competition. One of the reasons why we can purchase much better quality food or clothing for a much smaller portion of our income than our great grandparents would have thought possible is the cumulative effect of competition over the years.

Competition drove producers to find better, more comfortable textile materials that people could afford. Competition encouraged producers to offer shoppers more wholesome food, at lower prices. But being a monopoly, cumulative competition has never forced government to offer us more-for-less in the same way. No one in government is ever under pressure to offer the punters a two-for-one deal in order to stay in business.

Over the past thirty years, the costs of computing

have fallen dramatically. In 1956, one megabyte of computing power cost $10,000 in 1956 prices. In 2010, a megabyte cost 1/300th of 1 cent – and is still falling.[15] We are able to buy vastly more computing power for much less. Even if we do not purchase computers directly, as consumers we gain. As the costs of computing have fallen, banks, airlines and mobile phone companies have passed the lower administration costs on to us.

But not so when it comes to government administration. Think of your local hospital's administration costs, or the amount of time spent on paperwork in the local police station. Far from coming down, these kinds of administration costs have shot up.

Government is able to keep on sending us the bill for more government, which we have to pay on pain of going to prison. We have almost no consumer discretion over what services we get back in return. Unsurprisingly, the bill for government just keeps on growing.

'But so what,' I hear you say. 'Government might have grown, but it did so at a time when the West enjoyed an unprecedented rise in living standards.' Perhaps, you might even wonder, the growth of the former helps explain the increase in the latter?

It does not. The fact that one thing follows another does not mean that it was caused by it.

Government might have grown at a time of rapidly rising living standards, but more government did not make us more wealthy. More government is an extra claim on someone else's wealth, never additional wealth.

So how come government grew as the West got wealthy?

A massive expansion in Western economic output

over the past century allowed both an increase in living standards, *and enabled officialdom to grow by garnering greater resources.*

Like parasites, Western governments gorged themselves on the bounty of expanded economic output. The problem, as we shall see, is that they went even further, helping themselves to far more than many Western states produce, even after a century of rapidly expanded output.

ALPHABET SOUP GOVERNMENT

The more we spend on government, the more government we get – of that we can be certain. Less clear cut is whether we also get the services that we need.

Take education as an example. In return for a large slice of everyone's tax bill, government provides a school place for your children. But it is not only paying for Junior's classroom and the teachers who teach your child. You are not even just paying for the books or the teacher's pension or the hi-tech soft board that no British classroom seems able to cope without.

You are also paying for several thousand civil servants sitting in the Department for Education, and 80,000 administrative staff in England's publicly funded schools.[16] There are, according to Mark Steyn, more education officials in Britain today than teachers.[17]

You are buying a paraphernalia of education administrators, inspectors and regulators who will never set foot inside your child's classroom: OFQAL, OFSTED, the Training and Development Agency for Schools, something called Partnership for Schools. You are even paying for something called the Schools Food Trust.

With half our national income spent on government, it is impossible to pretend that officialdom is merely buying on your behalf all those services that you would otherwise have chosen anyhow. You are also being forced to pay for a bloated public administration that often has very little to do with any public services you might ever want.

In Britain there is so much of this extra officialdom around that we have even invented a term for it: quango (quasi-autonomous non-government organisation) government.

Often known by their acronym, quangos form a vast alphabet soup of officialdom; the ASA, DVLA, CQC ... There are so many quangos that officialdom is not even sure how many there are, with estimates between 766 and 1,148.[18] In fact in Britain there are so many government agencies and regulators, we have run out of letters of the alphabet to name them all. The letters FSA refer to both the Food Standards Agency, overseeing what we eat, and the Financial Services Authority, regulating our banks.

These executive agencies have executive powers, and are able to make rules that are statutorily binding – in other words have the effect of law. Let's fish just one single quango out of the soup, the Environment Agency. With a budget of £1,284 million and over 12,000 staff,[19] it issued thousands of pages of guidelines last year. From water abstraction licences to septic tank registration, its word tends to be final. For all practical effect, it decides the law on environmental policy, with, as we shall see, some much wider consequences for everyone else.

In the United States, there are dozens of federal

agencies housed in office buildings all over Washington
– the Anti-Trust Division, the Bureau of Industry, the
Centre for Nutrition ... The list is long. In fact, if we
Brits have difficulty finding enough abbreviations to
describe all this extra government, in the United States
there are at least four different federal agencies in the
US sharing the letters FSA. Perhaps it will not be long
before we will see the creation of a Government Agency
for the Allocation of Acronyms, or GAAA?

As in Britain, these agencies have enormous powers
to determine policy and make spending decisions.
Again, to pick a couple of examples at random: HUD, the
US federal housing agency, with an annual budget of $48
billion. Or Fannie Mae – the Federal National Mortgage
Association – which was once a public body accountable to Congress, but in 1968 became a publicly traded
company accountable to itself. Between them, HUD and
Fannie Mae not only spent billions of dollars making
public policy, they ran up enormous public liabilities
as they did so. While this was to have some pretty big
consequences for millions of Americans, there was
almost zero accountability to the American public on
the part of those making these decisions.

Japan, too, has its Administrative Evaluation Bureau,
the Administrative Management Bureau, the Local
Public Financial Bureau, the Local Administration
Bureau, the Local Tax Bureau and the Personnel and
Pension Bureau – in just one single Tokyo government
department.

Government is doing so much more than it says
on the tin, no one is certain what is inside the tin any
more. No one is really sure what all the letters on the
tin even stand for or what they do.

Buying more government has not simply given us more of the same. We have gone and bought ourselves a whole new way of being governed.

OVERGOVERNED

'Until August 1914', wrote the English historian AJP Taylor, an 'Englishman could pass through life and hardly notice the existence of the state ... He could live where he liked and as he liked ... broadly speaking, the state acted only to help those who could not help themselves. It left the adult citizen alone.'

You could not say the same of his great-grandchildren today. From the moment he gets out of bed in the morning, an Englishman's life is now supervised and regulated by government.

Government runs the energy market that supplies the electricity he uses as he switches on his bedside light. Government sets trade quotas through which the clothes he dresses in are imported. Government subsidises the sugar and the corn in his cereal bowl.

When an Englishman leaves home, he probably walks out of a home built in accordance with government directives. There is a one in five chance that he will work for government, but even if he runs a private business, he will have to work for the first five months of the year to pay for the taxes government takes from him.

All this extra government we pay for is not just cumbersome. It has changed what it means to be governed.

Back in 1914, people in Britain and America were governed by the legislative, executive and judicial branches of government, as described in text books. The laws that you had to obey were either passed by those you elected to the legislature, or else they came from the common law – the accumulated wisdom of court rulings down the years. The taxes you had to pay were levied by those you elected, either nationally or locally, too.

We are no longer ruled by those we elect. Instead we are ruled over by an activist bureaucracy. We are governed by the alphabet soup, with unelected officials in charge.

Beverly Smith,* a middle-aged mother in my Essex constituency, is no constitutional expert. But she learnt the hard way who really makes the rules in Britain today.

Concerned about proposals to build 140 new homes in her quiet rural village, she printed off a dozen or so leaflets on her home computer, inviting concerned residents to a meeting in the village hall. The meeting was well attended, and a team of residents was formed to try to have the new development scaled down.

Then out of the blue she got a letter from the alphabet soup, the ASA, or Advertising Standards Authority, threatening her with an unlimited fine.

For what exactly? The leaflets she printed off at home and placed, amongst other places, on the parish notice board, were an 'advertisement' apparently. Her 'advertisement' apparently contained 'inaccurate and misleading' information when it suggested that the new development might be bad for local wildlife.

Mr Greg Parker, the head of the ASA, demanded to know if she would 'withdraw' her misleading advertisement – or face an unlimited fine.

In other words, the ASA not only claims jurisdiction over every piece of paper printed off every home

* Name changed to protect identity.

computer and placed on every village notice board in England. But it claims the right to fine anyone who infringes its 'Code'.

Who drew up the ASA's 'Code'? Why, the ASA.

Who judges if Mrs Smith's village leaflets comply with the Code? According to section IV a) of the Code, the ASA's interpretation of its own Code is final.

So there you have it. The ASA makes rules that have the force of law. Interprets the rules that have the force of law. Can levy fines for non-compliance. But was elected by no one.

Free speech? The ASA claims the right to preside over what you print off in your own home, on your PC, when you invite local people to a meeting in the village hall claiming that too many homes in the village will be bad for the bluebells.

According to the ASA's Code, the ASA does not 'arbitrate between conflicting ideologies'. Yet it seems pretty prejudiced against the one that says it is none of Mr Parker's business to adjudicate on what Mrs Smith posts on the parish notice board – and that the law should be made by those Mrs Smith voted for.

But who can you vote for if you want to get Mr Parker out of office? You can't.

The Advertising Standards Authority can determine public policy, yet it does not answer to the public. It uses the force of law to insist that people comply with its rulings and regulation, and uses compulsion to collect a levy – a private tax revenue, if you like – on advertising and the postal service to raise its £7 million budget each year.

'In such a world, there is no "law",' writes Mark Steyn 'in the sense of a) you the citizen being found by b) a jury of your peers to be in breach of c) a statute passed by d) your elected representatives.'

Instead you are governed by 'unelected, unaccountable bureaucrats', able to 'determine transgressions, prosecute infractions, and levy fines for behavioural rules they themselves craft.'[20]

Businesses do not answer to customers, but to legions of officials. Companies in my Essex constituency keen to trade overseas tell me their greatest impediment is not finding overseas partners willing to buy, but British officialdom. A restaurant owner in Clacton tells me that he needed the permission of a dozen different statutory bodies to start up in business.

In 2005, the cost of complying with federal regulation in the United States was estimated to be $1.13 trillion – or 10 per cent of GDP.[21] It costs the US a tenth of national income to comply with all the rules and regulation being produced by the government Americans fund using 40 per cent of national income. In Britain, it is estimated that the cost of complying with red tape and regulation emanating from the European Union alone costs £20 billion each year – or some 2 per cent of GDP.[22]

When you buy as much government as the West now buys, you are not simply buying lots of super duper public services. You buy such a glut of extra government that eventually it begins to hamper the ability of the rest of society to generate enough wealth to pay for it all.

In America and Japan, the growth of government means that Congress and Parliament struggle to hold public administrators to account. In Europe, elected legislatures are not simply ineffective in holding the alphabet soup to account. The alphabet soup system has taken over.

Most law in Europe is now made by unelected government officials not in national capitals, but in the EU headquarters in Brussels. Agricultural policy, for example, is made by the European Commission's Directorate-General for Agriculture and Rural Development. Thirteen different mini-directorates churn out policy and directives on everything from farm support to the economics of the agricultural market.

'Supra-executive' administration in the West means that governments make a lot of rules without needing to pass laws. Government regulators pour forth regulations that do not emanate from elected legislatures. Government agencies issue guidelines that often assume statutory authority, without specifically being authorised in any Parliament, Assembly or Congress.

The more government we have, the less control the rest of us have over how government spends our money.

The more government has grown, the less say those who pay for it all have had over what they are getting in return for their money. We have bought so much additional public administration that it has outgrown the ability of representative democracy, with its legislatures and assemblies, to keep it all in check.

CHAPTER 2

WHY DOES GOVERNMENT GROW?

In 2009, Barack Obama pushed a $787 billion stimulus package through Congress, helping raise federal government spending as a share of GDP to 42 per cent – the highest level in US peacetime history. The package was passed on a knife-edge vote.

But try to imagine what might have happened if the cost of the Obama spending package had been divided up equally between each household, and the $9,539[23] bill posted out to every American home.

It is not only the Tea Party movement that would have been protesting. Opposition to the package would have been fierce and mainstream, not just fierce and fringe.

The previous year, British Prime Minister Gordon Brown announced a £500 billion bank bailout, with a £37 billion direct injection of taxpayer money. Unlike Obama, he did not even need to put it to a vote in Parliament first.

Criticism was muted, with only occasional backbench Members of Parliament, like me, questioning the wisdom of bailout-and-borrow economics.

Yet imagine what the response might have been if every British adult had been sent an invoice the following day for the £1,028[24] cost of the bank bailout. Imagine how MPs might have reacted then.

To pose these questions is to get a sense of what once kept government small. Because the bill for more government was divided proportionately amongst voters, voters tended to elect representatives who were careful with their tax cash.

The link between taxation and representation is the key to understanding what can keep government small.

DELIBERATELY LIMITED GOVERNMENT

'No taxation without representation!' yelled the American rebels. Theirs was the cry of people who understood the link between how you vote and what you pay for.

Yet the New England rebels of the 1770s were echoing the demands of the old English parliamentary cause in the 1640s. And the English rebels of the seventeenth century were reiterating an idea of limited government that had been articulated even earlier.

As far back as 1100, if not even centuries before,[25] the powers of English kings had been deliberately constrained. Henry I presented a Charter of Liberties in which he set limits on his power. A century later, Magna Carta not only limited the power of a king; it was pressure from below that was defining the scope of King John's power, no longer the Crown itself.

When in 1628 English Parliamentarians presented a Petition of Right to King Charles I, they did so by invoking ancient English statutes from the time of Edward I, which, they claimed, required that Parliament's consent was obtained before taxes could be levied. The English

Civil War that followed was fought to assert, as much as
to establish, such rights.

Charles I's defeat left Parliament with power
over taxation. 'No man', proclaimed the victorious
Parliamentarians, might 'hereafter be compelled to
make or yield any tax without common consent by act
of Parliament'.

Awkwardly and clumsily, seventeenth-century
England stumbled towards a constitutional settlement
that would enshrine the supremacy of Parliament,
arriving there eventually with the Glorious Revolution
of 1688. The Bill of Rights that followed explicitly
limited the power of government.

When the American rebels prevailed at Yorktown a
hundred years or so later, they too tried to put in place
constitutional arrangements that would deliberately
constrain the power of government. And in many
respects theirs was a far more successful attempt than
that made by their English cousins.

The Constitution that the American Founding
Fathers drew up for their fledgling republic is perhaps
the greatest attempt yet made to limit the power of
government. This extraordinary document carefully
disperses power, separating it between state and
federal levels, between executive, legislative and judicial branches, setting in place checks and balances.

Yet the document that the Founding Fathers drew
up in an old court house in Philadelphia during the
summer of 1787 was not merely a product of their
long deliberations. It was but the latest step on
a long road towards limited government, which had
started on the other side of the Atlantic. Far from a
revolutionary cry, when Americans demanded 'No

taxation without representation', they believed they were asserting a long-established claim, one that had been temporarily usurped by a tyrannical king. The Constitution they devised used representative institutions to safeguard rights that they held to be inalienable.

Politicians might today be seen as expropriators for more government. But the parliaments and legislatures in which they sit came into being in the first place to ensure the precise opposite: to prevent monarchs or ministers from levying taxes without the consent of the people.

Representative government was designed to keep government small.

DON'T BLAME DEMOCRACY

'Wrong, Carswell,' you say. 'Everybody knows that government got big because of democracy. As the vote was extended to the masses, government became representative of the masses to the point it started to act on their behalf and redistribute wealth.'

I have often heard this point asserted, but seldom made.

The idea that government grew big because of democracy is a myth. For a start, the chronology does not fit.

Look at America. Almost every white adult male had had the vote since the era of Jacksonian democracy in the 1830s and 1840s. Yet throughout the whole of the nineteenth century, federal spending as a percentage of US GDP never once rose above 3 per cent of GDP during peacetime.

Can you point to a time when the massed ranks of

American voters in the nineteenth century voted for big government? Me neither.

Not only did the American electorate not vote for a redistributive state, they decisively rejected it when it was offered to them.

Consider what happened in the 1890s, for example. Between 1893 and 1896, the United States experienced a catastrophic depression – deeper and more severe than anything until the Great Depression of the 1930s.

The stock exchange crashed. Some 18 per cent of the workforce was out of work. In 1893, 15,000 businesses failed. Seven hundred banks went under. A sixth of railroad companies went bust. America's GDP fell 7 per cent that year, and then 5 per cent the year after.

How did the enfranchised masses vote? Did they opt for the explicitly redistributionist policies offered by the Populists, and their charismatic leader, William Jennings Bryan? Did they rally to those proposing federal intervention in agriculture and the economy?

Not at all. The point about the Populists is that they were not very popular. Fearful of having to foot the bill, the electorate decisively and repeatedly rejected their redistributive platform, with Bryan losing three elections in a row.

Instead the voters installed in the White House Grover Cleveland, a man who seemed to embody the ideal of limited government.[26]

As the English observer of America, James Pryce, noted not long afterwards, 'Poorer citizens have long been a numerical majority, invested with political power ... One might have feared the poor would have thrown the burden of taxation upon the rich ... not only has this not been attempted, it has scarcely been suggested.'

Nor does the chronology fit the democracy-leads-to-Big-Government theory in Europe, either.

Every Frenchman got the right to vote after 1848. Yet where was the increase in the size of the French state in the years that followed? The amount of public expenditure on, for example, public education actually fell. Government did less after the extension of the franchise than in the decades before.

England, too, was more democratic at the end of the nineteenth century than she had been at the beginning. But did this lead to a more redistributive state?

It turns out that the opposite was the case. In the 1870s and 1880s, England's poor laws redistributed a smaller share of national income than they had during the first two decades of the nineteenth century. More democracy seemed to be accompanied by a less redistributive state.

But perhaps those who lazily claim that Big Government is a product of democracy have the biggest difficulty explaining Prussia.

Prussia was the least democratic Western state for most of the nineteenth century. Unlike the House of Commons, or the US Congress, which were designed to be representative institutions, Prussia's bicameral legislatures – the Herrenhaus and Abgeordnetenhaus – allocated voting shares to the electorate to ensure the predominance of the elite. Far from representative government, Prussia's political arrangements were intended to prevent popular pressure from the working man below.

Yet Prussia pioneered the idea of interventionist government.

In 1881, Germany was the first state in the world

to legislate for social insurance in case of accidents, in 1883 for sickness insurance, and in 1889 for old age insurance.

It is not credible to suggest that Otto von Bismarck did any of this in response to the demands of a newly enfranchised electorate. No such mass electorate existed. His reforms were instead introduced at the behest of highly educated, elite social reformers, men like Theodor Lohmann. The interventionist state in Germany, as elsewhere, turns out to have been a product of an activist elite, not the enfranchised masses.

In truth, elite opinion in nineteenth-century Britain often suggested that government ought to do more, too. As early as the 1780s, Jeremy Bentham and the utilitarians had advocated that government and the law should no longer merely guarantee individuals their freedoms and property, but be an instrument for change.

Victorian public administrators such as Nassau Senior and Edwin Chadwick sought to make government a player, rather than a spectator, in social and economic affairs. There were no shortage of social reformers in late Victorian Britain who looked on with admiration at the 'Prussian model'.

But the point is that they were prevented from emulating such a model by Parliament. The arrangements put in place to limit the role and size of government worked. Representative government remained small.

As Walter Bagehot put it at the time, 'the best safeguard against excessive taxation' is parliamentary sensitivity to public opinion.[27] With voters in Britain and America having to pay the tax bill, Parliament and Congress remained hyper-sensitive to proposals for even the most modest tax rises.

'But what about the extension of the franchise in Britain in 1867 and 1884?' you might wonder. 'Surely it was this that led to demands for government to do more?'

Of course the Reform Acts of 1867 and 1884 widened the electoral franchise. But even after the working man got the vote, because of the way that taxes were levied, the newly enfranchised masses still stood to pay a proportionate share of the tax bill. And because they stood to get the tax bill, they still tended to elect representatives to Parliament inclined to keep the bill – and therefore government – small.

Years, even decades, after the extension of the franchise, Victorian politics remained a contest between competing claims for thrift and prudence with public money.

It was not extending the franchise in the late nineteenth century that made representative institutions less inclined to rein in government. Rather it was changes to the tax base in the early twentieth century, which started to mean that voters no longer got sent the bill for how they voted.

'But what about the history of the 1930s?' you retort, leaping ahead half a century. 'During that decade the notion that government should be more interventionist won hands down. Government not only got bigger, but bigger government proved widely popular in Britain and America.'

During the New Deal, President Roosevelt did indeed make the kind of interventions in the US economy that William Jennings Bryan could once have only dreamed of. Across the Atlantic, the British government discarded the gold standard and adopted a system that left politicians managing the money – something Bryan advocated back in the 1890s.

Government grew much bigger in the democratic West during the 1930s, of that there is no doubt. But it grew even bigger in *non-democratic* Western states during that decade.

However interventionist Roosevelt's New Deal, 1930s America was nothing like as *dirigiste* as Hitler's Germany, with its massive government programmes designed to achieve full employment and a national socialist economy. However decisively Britain might have moved away from the nineteenth-century, *laissez-faire* Victorian ideal, she was nothing like as statist as Italy under Mussolini.

The history of the 1930s shows that government tended to grow larger where democratic constraints were weaker. If anything, democratic constraints pre-vented Roosevelt and Britain's National Government from being even more interventionist.

Democracy constrains the growth of government, it does not drive it.

'But what about Britain's post-war generation voting for the welfare state? Surely voters *did* choose Big Government?' you insist.

No one disputes that Labour leader Clement Attlee won the 1945 general election handsomely. But when-ever voters have voted for more government – as they undoubtedly have – it has usually happened when a large slice of the electorate believe that it is not they who will be paying for it.

No matter how many people might be allowed to vote, as long as everyone is made to pay a propor-tionate share of the tax bill, the majority do not vote to expropriate from a minority. It was not the equal distribution of voting rights that changed things, but the unequal distribution of the tax bill. Once the tax bill is no longer divided up proportionately, expropriation became almost inevitable.

So how was it possible to divide up the tax bill unequally? How could the true cost of more government be kept from the voters so as to persuade enough voters to vote for it? By concealing it.

CONCEALING THE COSTS OF GOVERNMENT

Of course, an invoice for Barack Obama's stimulus package or Gordon Brown's bank bailout never did get posted out to every home.

So what did happen to the bill?

The money was raised through a three-card trick involving higher income taxes on a small minority, more borrowing, and printing money.

Income tax means that the burden of taxation is spread out unequally amongst voters. Some voters get to appreciate the higher costs of more government more than others.

Borrowing means that in the short term, voters are unaware of the increased costs of extra government. Western governments have simply borrowed on such a vast, extravagant scale that they have, in effect, been spending without taxing.

Finally, by manipulation of our money, government has been able to subtly transfer resources from us to it, without people really being aware of what is going on.

The costs of the Obama stimulus or the Brown bailouts might not have been billed to us directly. But they will be as real in the end as if they had been.

Through a combination of unequal tax, extra borrowing and monetary manipulation, the costs of all that extra government were concealed. The sums are there on government websites for anyone wanting to take a look, but most people will not feel the real financial burden of those increased costs quite yet.

This, in essence, is why Western governments have been able to grow. The unwillingness of voters to pay additional taxes kept government small. But once government figured out a way to conceal those costs from enough of the electorate, the reticence evaporated.

INCOME TAX

Have you ever gone out to a restaurant with a group of colleagues after work? Imagine that there were a dozen or so of you sat round the table. How did you divide the bill at the end of the evening?

Perhaps you asked the geeky guy from accounts to calculate who ate what, and divide it that way. Or perhaps you decided to ignore how two or three colleagues shared a bottle of wine, while you had none, and just split the bill equally between everyone.

But what do you think might have happened if at the start of the meal, your boss had said that the company was going to be picking up the tab for everyone?

My guess is that when choosing from the menu, some of your colleagues might have opted for the expensive steak. You would have decided to go for three courses, not just the two. If you weren't all going to have to pay a proportionate share of the bill, the bill would most likely be higher.

That is what has happened with taxation.

The bill for government has grown big because many of those sitting round the table deciding what to have are not having to pay for it.

In America, one in ten people pay 55 per cent of the income tax bill. Just under half of households pay no income tax at all. In Britain, one in ten people pay nearly 60 per cent of the bill.

It did not always use to be this way.

In eighteenth- and nineteenth-century Britain, for example, the main source of government revenue came from property taxes – notably a uniform land tax. Of course, the more land you owned, the more you paid. But the burden was proportionate. Richer people might pay more, but the percentage remained the same. The yeoman farmer paid proportionately the same as the toff with his vast estate.

Indeed, if you stop and think about it, it would have been remarkably difficult to have it any other way. So long as you are taxing people for the property they have, or taxing them for what they consume, it is rather difficult to charge person X a higher rate than person Y. You cannot easily levy a higher rate of tax on that extra acre someone owns, or raise the rate of sales tax on their second shopping trolley. It is taxing *income* that makes unequal, or disproportionate, taxation possible.

It was the invention of disproportionate taxation – which had to mean a tax on income – that made the growth of Big Government possible. Disproportionate taxes are, as Louis XIV's finance minister might have put it, a remarkably clever way of 'plucking the goose to obtain the largest amount of feathers with the smallest amount of hissing'.

Although introduced as a temporary measure during

the Napoleonic wars in Britain, and briefly again in the 1840s, the graduated system of income tax we have today was not introduced in Britain until 1907–09. Income tax was introduced in Australia by 1907, the United States in 1913 and Canada in 1917. In every case, Big Government soon followed.

Within a few years of the introduction of income tax, the amount that governments spent as a share of GDP began to rise. It has never really stopped rising.

US distribution of income

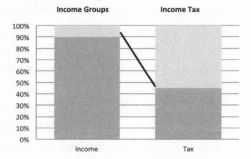

Source: US Tax Policy Centre, Table T11-0091 and HMRC Statistics, Table 2.4

Income tax has allowed government to grow because it raises a lot of money. Today income tax is often the single largest source of government income, accounting for about 65 per cent of Australian federal government income and almost half the US federal government's earning, and it is the UK government's single largest revenue stream.

But far more significant than the extra revenue it generated, a graduated income tax has enabled the cost of more government to be raised without provoking a backlash.

Take Britain's Prime Minister David Lloyd George, and his 1909 People's Budget. It was Britain's first explicitly redistributionist budget, provoking great controversy. For all the drama and crisis, however, it passed through Parliament, in large measure because Lloyd George had made it clear that the average workman would have to pay no income tax at all.

Ten years on, however, and what had happened? The average workman was paying a seventh of his gross earnings in income tax.

How popular with the people do you think the People's Budget would have been if it had proposed that level of taxation at the outset? The *People's* Budget? They would have loathed it. But raise the burden incrementally, and somehow what seems like an intolerable burden just sort of happens.

In the early 1930s, fewer than ten million Americans paid federal income tax. By the late 1940s, over fifty million did. A graduated income tax allowed an extra forty million Americans to be drawn into the income tax system with little political opposition – and without which the colossal increase in the size of the federal government in the 1930s would not have been possible.

Or what about Barack Obama's 2009 Budget – the modern American equivalent of the People's Budget? With 47 per cent of US households paying no federal income tax at all,[28] of course the balance of opinion inside Congress – and outside – was much less hostile to such largesse with other people's money than it would otherwise have been. Half the people sitting round the table are happy to order steak because they know they will not be paying.

Today in Britain 3.7 million people now pay what

would have once been regarded as an eye-watering 40 per cent rate of income tax.[29] Perhaps when your richer neighbour started paying 40 per cent tax rates a few years back, you assumed that only rich people would have to pay. Now you find that you have drifted into that same tax bracket, but it feels like you are the only one outraged about it. Imagine if government had instead demanded you, your neighbour and everyone else pay a 40 per cent tax bill at the same time.

Parliamentary or Congressional sensitivity to public opinion used to keep government spending down. But that can only work if the people are themselves sensitive to higher state spending.

Dividing up the burden of taxation unequally means that a significant slice of the electorate is desensitised to the cost of more government. Some geese might hiss some of the time, but the graduated rate of taxation ensures that as you pluck them in turn, not all the geese hiss at the same time.

Perhaps this explains why the more unequal the tax burden is, the higher the overall tax burden gets to be.

In the United States, income tax rates range from 10 to 35 per cent, and the federal government spends 40 per cent of GDP. In France, where the state accounts for 57 per cent of national income, the bands stretch from 5.5 to 40 per cent.[30] In Britain, government is a little smaller than in France, and income tax bands range a little less, from 20 to 45 per cent. It is not the correlation between the higher rate of tax and the size of government that is most striking. Rather it is the fact that where income tax rates vary most between the top rate and the bottom rate, government tends to be biggest. The more unequally the tax burden is spread, the easier it is for government to grow.

Today in Britain the richest 10 per cent pay 53 per cent of all income tax. In the United States, one in every five dollars raised in federal revenue is contributed by a mere 1 per cent of the taxpaying population. The top 20 per cent of earners earn 55 per cent of income, yet contribute 70 per cent of all taxes.

None of this should surprise us. The idea that graduated income tax has allowed government to grow can hardly be called controversial. Indeed, those who demanded the new system of taxation at the turn of the nineteenth century never did so merely to raise more revenue. They called for a graduated income tax as a necessary step towards changing the role of government in society, too – and they said as much at the time.

They understood that adding more people to the electoral roll had not enabled government to tax and spend more. They recognised that the key to getting more government was to divide the bill for it up unequally by getting your neighbour to pay for it.

If income tax enables government to grow by passing the bill to your neighbour, public borrowing enables government to grow by passing the bill to your children – and to your children's children.

SPENDING WITHOUT TAXATION

Just like households or businesses, governments need to be able to borrow. This is not necessarily a bad thing.

It was the ability to borrow on the newly emerged capital markets that allowed both Western businesses and governments to prosper. Capital markets enabled

Holland and England to prevail in their seventeenth-century struggles with Spain and France by enabling them to mobilise resources more effectively than their bigger neighbours. Being able to borrow enables a state to meet costs that must be met right away – without getting sunk by cashflow constraints in the process.

The trouble is that Western governments no longer borrow the way they once did.

In previous centuries, government borrowing was paid for out of taxation. The more bonds a government issued to meet costs, the higher the tax rate. Relatively small increases in public debt proved extraordinarily (by contemporary standards) controversial precisely because of the tax rises that would need to follow to repay the loan.

Today, Western governments are no longer meaningfully accountable to elected legislatures for how much they borrow. Most of it is done by executive fiat. Instead of asking the permission of your elected representatives before spending money, government in most Western states meets the costs not only out of direct taxes, but by issuing bits of paper called government bonds.

Nor do governments tend to pay back the costs of the loan out of taxation directly the way they did. Old debts are typically recycled as new debts, new bonds issued to replace maturing ones.

Instead of borrowing out of necessity – to meet unexpected costs that could not be otherwise met from current tax revenue – Western governments now routinely borrow to pay for current consumption. It has become the political equivalent of supplementing your monthly income by putting your grocery bill on a credit card. Far from allowing government to deal with unexpected contingencies, it has become a way of enabling officialdom to carry on living beyond the means of the rest of us to pay for it.

For every £6 that the British government spends over the next year, it is expected to borrow £1. For every $5 the United States government spends, it is expected to borrow $1. Japan's government has been spending more each year than she collects in taxes for so long, you need to go back almost a quarter of a century to find a time when she did not.

Imagine if you ran your finances that way. What if for every £100 you spent on household items each month, you borrowed £20? That is the way Western public finances – with a few exceptions such as Finland, Germany and Australia – have been run to pay for government for a generation.

How have governments been able to get away with it for so long? If it is so obvious, why have we not put an end to it?

In part, reality has been avoided by simply rolling over the debt – the equivalent of taking out a new credit card to pay off the debts on the old.

But partly government has been able to avoid reality because of what happens once it has issued those bonds.

The government sells its bonds to corporate banks, exchanging the paper IOUs for money government can then spend.

'But surely', you think, 'the banks would eventually say "enough"?'

That would seem obvious, until you realise the other side of the transaction that is taking place. At the same time as swapping money for bonds with government, corporate banks trade those bonds for more money from the central bank, which the central bank more or less prints out of thin air. Why call time on a series of transactions that make you rich?

Between them, governments, central banks and banks have been able to conjure up money and credit from nothing. This helps governments to fund the shortfall in government taxes. And, of course, the banks rather like all that extra credit, which they can then lend on at a profit.

'But how is this possible?' you might ask. 'That cannot really be the way that the Western money system is run.'

It never used to be. But it is now.

As well as issuing all those IOU bonds denominated in dollars or pounds or yen, government also controls the supply of dollars, pounds and yen. It can manipulate the money system in which its debts are measured.

Only recently have Western governments begun to fund their spending habits in this way. Governments had been engineering inflation to their advantage ever since the suspension of the gold standard at the outbreak of the First World War. But they did not begin to do so systematically during peacetime until forty years ago.

Until 1971, the amount of US dollars put into circulation was linked to the amount of gold the US Treasury held. Most other Western currencies were linked to the US dollar. Far removed from the classic gold standard, this so-called Bretton Woods system nonetheless meant that Western governments could not simply print off whatever amount of currency they wanted to.

Since the collapse of Bretton Woods, how much money there is in circulation in America, Britain, Europe and Japan has been determined by government. Government not only issues the debt, but controls the supply of the currency in which the debt is denominated.

'But', you persist, 'you cannot magic away the costs of all that government spending. Someone must surely be paying for it?'

And someone does. There is a victim. And that victim is you – and every other citizen.

If you have a bank account with lots of pounds or dollars in it, and the government then goes and prints lots more pounds or dollars, the value for the ones that you have gets smaller. Or, looked at another way, your pounds or dollars are able to buy less, as prices rise.

This is called inflation – and inflation is built into our modern monetary system. That governments have inflation targets is a reflection of the way they set out to debauch the value of the currency over time. Western finance ministers even get together every few months to agree what their inflation targets are going to be, synchronising the rate at which they debase their currencies internally to prevent wholesale external devaluations between currencies.

Inflation is a tax that you have to pay in order to fund all that extra government that you never actually voted for. And which you might well not have voted for if you had ever been asked. But that is precisely the point. It is a form of cost concealment that allows government to grow big at your expense without your say-so.

Not surprisingly, since 1971, the dollar has lost approximately 80 per cent of its value, the British pound 90 per cent of its value and the Japanese yen about half its value.[31] At the same time, government spending in the United States has risen almost four fold,[32] and government spending in Britain and Japan has more than doubled.[33]

The Swiss franc, by comparison, was for most of the past century backed by gold. That meant that before the Swiss state could circulate any extra money, it had to have 40 per cent of the value of the extra money held in gold in a bank vault. This acted as a brake on the amount of money the Swiss state printed, and the Swiss franc lost only about a fifth of its value over the same period.

So guess what? Unable to print money to pay for things, the Swiss state has remained pretty small. The size of government in Switzerland has risen from 29 per cent of GDP to 34 per cent over all that time – a minor hiccup by comparison.

A policy of deliberate inflation of 2–3 per cent each year might not sound much, but cumulatively, it has an enormous impact. Since 1990, Britain for example has had average inflation of about 3 per cent. The compound effect means that what you could have bought for £100 in 1990 you would today need £196 to buy.

Since 1971, there have been fierce debates about what monetary policy should be, and how much money government should put into circulation. But whether it is monetarists (who want less money in circulation) or Keynesians (who tend to prefer putting more money into circulation), somehow monetary policy always seems to be run in the interests of government, banks and central bankers – not the public.

Perhaps I should also point to one final trick that government has up its sleeve in order to grow without having to run the bill past you first. It is a form of never-never debt financing.

In Britain, vast PFI – or Public Finance Initiative – projects have extended public liabilities way beyond conventional borrowing on the bond markets. In America they are called Public/Private Partnerships, but the principle is the same. Fancy a new school, hospital or ship for the navy? Whack it on the PFI credit card. Have the contractor deliver it now, and worry about who will have to service the 25-year debt repayments later.

According to the Conservative MP Brooks Newmark, these hidden 'off-balance sheet' liabilities now total over 20 per cent of total GDP, or £11,330 of debt per household in Britain – on top of the £32,000 of official debt you already knew about.[34] It is no different to discovering that a feckless husband has been running up a massive debt on a credit card that he kept hidden from his wife. Ever wondered where all those nice gifts government wowed you with came from? That's right. They were paid for on that credit card you never knew about. You will know about it soon enough when you start getting payment demands from the bailiffs.

DEBAUCHED DEMOCRACY

As I type this in the House of Commons, I am sitting a few yards from the spot where an earlier generation of Parliamentarians defied Charles I, refusing to pay him ship money.

The King demanded taxation without the approval

of those elected to Parliament by those expected to pay for it all. Parliament refused. They fought a civil war over it, and cut the King's head off across the street when he lost.

Three hundred and seventy years later, the House of Commons is still there. Elected MPs are still there. Elections still happen. It is just that government has worked out how to raise a lot more than ship money without needing to get the approval of those who have to pay for it.

The constitutional arrangements that were put in place in the seventeenth century to keep government small have proved inadequate at doing so in the early twenty-first century.

When on October 8 2008, Britain's Chancellor of the Exchequer announced a £500 billion bank bailout he was telling MPs, not asking. There was no vote to approve the decision in the Commons. The announcement made in Parliament was precisely that – a declaration of what had been done. It was done by the kind of executive decree that Charles I would have died for. And indeed did.

Watching it, I caught sight of what Britain would be like had Charles I won his battle to raise ship money, rather than lose his head. Officials would be able to make billion-pound tax and spending decisions without reference to those we elect. Yet to my horror, I realised on that cold, dreary afternoon in Westminster that is precisely what now happens.

The entire purpose of having a parliament is to approve how government spends public money. Yet a £500 billion decision can today be taken without a proper debate. It is officials in the Treasury building in Whitehall – almost opposite the exact spot where Charles was executed – that decide what taxes we pay and where taxes are spent.

Parliamentarians have meekly handed away the powers over tax and supply which their forebears fought and died to obtain.

Since the 1930s, Estimates Days in the Commons have become a routine mechanism to approve how much government spends. MPs have not had the ability to table amendments to, or try to alter in any way, the estimates put in front of them. Parliamentary approval is required – but it is a formality.

Budget Day in Westminster is a day of ritual. While nothing as grand as the Queen's State Opening of Parliament, with its horse-drawn carriages and cavalry, it has about as much practical purpose. Just as the Queen reads a speech scripted for her by others, on Budget Day politicians debate tax-and-spend decisions that have been determined by unelected officials.

Remarkably few MPs even realise what is in the Budgets they vacuously 'debate'. In March 2007, despite over twelve hours discussing the Budget, it took many, if not most, MPs almost a full year to appreciate that what they had just rubber stamped would double the income tax rate of the poorest taxpayers.

The reality is that tax-and-spend decisions are made by officials in the Treasury. Government departments and all those supra-executive agencies are allocated their budget by officials. Parliamentary approval of government agency spending is not even required.

Government in Britain – and much of Europe – has grown big precisely because elected legislatures no longer have the power to control what government spends. In seventeen Eurozone countries, elected legislatures are only allowed to even debate budgets that have already been approved and signed off by unelected Euro officials.

That government in America is smaller than in Britain is perhaps a reflection of the fact that Congress still retains greater powers to say 'no' to more government. Ten days before Britain's Parliament was told about a £500 billion rescue bailout, Congress approved a $700 billion rescue for US banks. But unlike the British bailout, the American rescue package was debated for many hours. Amendments were tabled and argued over. Approval only came when assurances had been given and parts of the rescue package watered down.

And yet approval for the US bailout was still given.

Concealing the costs of government through income tax, borrowing and money manipulation breaks the link between taxation and representation. Once voters no longer pay directly for the kind of government that they vote for, democracy is debauched. Purpose drains away from those assemblies and legislatures that once existed to keep government small.

For as long as voters have to pay for the costs of government, they will tend to elect representatives who will be careful with their tax money. Politics will almost always be a competition to be thrifty, and to obtain the best value out of any budget.

But once the costs of government are no longer

paid directly and proportionately by voters, politics becomes a Dutch auction of promises.

DON'T BLAME THE WAR

Government grew in size, we are often told, because of war. Or because of various crises and emergencies.

It is undoubtedly true. Many of the big increases in the size of the state happened in times of war. Government spending rose dramatically in most Western states during the First and Second World Wars – and in many Western states, but by no means all, remained larger than it had been before the war. It was during the two world wars that governments established economic controls, which were not always relinquished in the peace that followed.

Economic crisis, too, saw government expand. It was during the Great Depression of the 1930s that the federal government in America expanded most dramatically. More recently, Western governments have grown again in response to the financial crisis since 2007.

It is much easier for governments to spend money they do not have in times of crisis. The democratic safeguards can be suspended – sometimes temporarily, often permanently. It was, for example, during the 1930s – a time of crisis that called for a National Government – that the House of Commons rule book was changed, leaving MPs able to do no more than rubber-stamp spending decisions. All that parliamentary debate, counselled fashionable opinion in those troubled times, was getting in the way of the need to act swiftly.

A crisis demands action. Or as Barack Obama's White House chief of staff, Rahm Emanuel, put it, 'Never let a serious crisis go to waste. It's an opportunity to do things you could not do before.'

The New Deal saw Roosevelt circumvent a whole series of constitutional safeguards designed to prevent the federal government from doing many of the things that he did. In the climate of the time, the need for action – almost any action – prevailed. Indeed, so much so that the early New Deal is full of incoherent – even contradictory – ideas.

Urgency means normal rules can be set aside. During the banking crisis in Britain in 2008, competition rules were brushed aside to allow the merger of HBOS and RBS.

War and crises often tell us *how* government grew, not necessarily *why* government grew.

War and crises remove the constraints. They remove the brakes. But claiming that a car moves forward because the brakes have been taken off does not fully explain why the car is propelled forward. Removing the brakes might allow a car to travel forward – but it is the engine inside the car that drives it.

So, too, with the growth of government.

Taking off the brakes allows Big Government to grow. But it is the engine of statism that actually motors the expansion of government.

War and crises free the technocratic elite in society to act without constraint. When government expands during wartime and crisis, it is doing so because those who believe that social and economic affairs can best be arranged by deliberate design are given a free hand – and a large amount of money – to get on with it. It is this – the engine of statism – that drives forward Big Government when the brakes are off.

CHAPTER 3

THE ENGINE OF STATISM

Government has employed more and more ambitious elites able to capture a greater and greater share of societies' income by interfering more and more in people's lives as they give themselves more and more rules to enforce, until they kill the goose that lays the golden eggs.
Matt Ridley, *The Rational Optimist*

1 884, imply the school text books, was the year that Big Government in Britain began. That was when William Gladstone's Reform Act gave the English working man the vote – and government has grown by popular demand ever since.

1884 was indeed a key milestone in the growth of Big Government. But not because the extension of the right to vote unleashed demands for greater government from below. Rather, it was the year in which the Fabian Society was formed, a key milestone in the demand for Big Government *from above*.

Of course, it wasn't just the Fabians. They were just one manifestation of the rise of this new class of intellectuals. Late Victorian and early Edwardian Britain were awash with social reformers of one sort or another. Across the Atlantic the so-called Progressives represented much the same sort of elitist phenomenon.

In Britain, it was this new elite, not the newly enfranchised working man, who demanded that Britain emulate Prussia's social statism and who called for a graduated income tax. It was intellectuals like AC Pigou who demanded a redistributive state, or who later, like John Maynard Keynes, called for the end of *laissez-faire*. It was the voice of Harold Laski, not the working man, urging 'an aristocracy of delegation'.

Demands for more government came not from below, but from above.

THE INFLUENCE OF THE ELITE

How did you hear about the banking crisis? Who told you about climate change, or the meltdown in the Eurozone?

What we learn about current affairs and the wider world tends to come to us via journalists. Good news or bad, it is often a media commentator who explains to us what has gone right – or more often, wrong. Maybe it was a university professor, a teacher or an expert academic who helped to explain why things turned out that way – and by implication what needed to be done about it. Perhaps it was then a politician or public official who discussed how government needed to respond.

If you stop to think about it, so much of what we hear about the wider world is filtered to us via a remarkably small number of people. Intellectuals, you might call them. Or to use a term coined by the Austrian-born thinker and philosopher, Friedrich Hayek, the 'second-hand dealers in ideas'.

Hayek, who lived and taught throughout Europe,

Britain and America during the last century, identified the role such people play in disseminating ideas and defining the terms of public policy debate in contemporary Western society in his groundbreaking 1949 essay, 'Intellectuals and Socialism'.

As Hayek made plain, these 'secondhand dealers in ideas' need not be particularly intelligent. Those of the species I have come across during my time in the Westminster village – the media pundits, ministers and mandarins – often tend not to be particularly original thinkers at all. However bright or academically gifted, a reputation of genuine independence of thought is more likely to hinder, not help, a career amongst such people.

Our political and media illuminati are to new ideas what the moon is to sunlight. However brightly they might shine, they only ever do so by reflecting what emanates from elsewhere. Few ever radiate new ideas the way the sun radiates its own light, but merely throw back what happens to be around them. Thus is so much of the Westminster village dimly lit by secondhand thinking.

This small elite decide from what angle an event is presented to the rest of us. They frame the terms of the debate, and decide which opinions will be heard – and who will not be heard.[35] In Britain, it was the BBC's Robert Peston who informed the public about the bank bailouts in 2008. Several years on, he is pronouncing about the bailout of entire countries.

Peston and Co. act as gatekeepers of information – in his case literally, his insider contacts phoning him with scoops. It is such secondhand dealers in other people's ideas who analyse economic news and current affairs, and explain even our history and our past. All too often they seem to tell the rest of us what must be done in the future, too.

This elite are to our world what priests and princes would have been to the medieval masses; they interpret the world, explain events and at times claim an authority to decide what happens next.

Western states are democracies in the sense that the masses have the ability to mark a ballot paper every few years. But it is the elite, the politicians, civil servants, business leaders and newspaper editors – what you might term the 'official mind' – think that matters. It is the 'official mind' that determines what governments actually do. And it is Hayek's secondhand dealers in ideas that usually decide what the 'official mind' thinks.

THE CONCEITED ELITE

The ideas of economists and political philosophers, both when they are right and when they are wrong, are more powerful than is commonly understood.
John Maynard Keynes

We all like the idea of the elite 'expert': the disinterested class of specialist who, like Plato's guardians, can raise their eyes above the partisan scrum and descry the common interest. The trouble is that such a class of elite experts does not exist. We all have our prejudices and presumptions, and the elite more than most.

Throughout the West, the elite exhibit a consistent bias in favour of top-down, *dirigiste* decision making. A small number of people deciding what is right for the many.

Listen carefully next time education experts discuss the 'right' way to teach a child. Or public officials talk about the 'right' kind of development in your town. Or regulators discuss the 'right' way to structure banking. Or politicians talk about the 'right' way to achieve economic growth.

Whatever particular proposal they seem to be making, the key point is that they are presuming that the policy ought to be a matter of public policy in the first place. That everyone should abide by what is deemed 'right'.

When those educationalists tell us what they believe is the best way to educate a child, they are not saying that is how they will therefore be teaching their kids. They are demanding the right to decide what is right for everybody else's. When a public official talks about the right kind of urban planning, they are not proposing to build their home that way. They want to do so for lots of other people.

Each time a regulator claims that they know how to run a bank, they are not proposing to run their own bank that way. They want to tell everyone else how to do it. And when a politician starts tell us what the right sort of economic growth looks like, they are not actually about to start generating wealth themselves, just presuming to know how others should do so.

When our technocratic elite debate public policy, they are almost always arguing over what constitutes the best design. Which blueprint. What kind of regulation. What shape for national policy. The presumption is always that there must be a design.

This presumption in favour of doing things by design is so commonplace we perhaps take it for granted. But it is worth asking why it is that public officials almost always want more public officialdom.

Far from being disinterested, all bureaucracies and bureaucrats have institutional tendencies and inclinations. They possess what the French term *déformation professionelle*: outlooks and attitudes skewed by career imperatives.

Federal officials working at the Federal Housing Agency will tend to favour more money to support federal housing projects. Eurocrats in Brussels will tend to favour more Brussels. Those at the Department for International Development will tend to favour more government-to-government aid spending.

If different public agencies and experts each have their own specific inclinations, there is one overarching bias amongst almost all public officials: a tendency to believe that public officials should be determining things for us by design in the first place.

Why is this?

It is a prejudice born of a fallacy: the mistaken belief that perfect knowledge can be assembled in one place or concentrated in a single spot. Usually in the office where a public official sits. Or in the studio from where the media experts pontificate.

To use Hayek's terminology, the elite are 'constructive rationalists' – they believe that progress comes via top-down, conscious design. Like the seventeenth-century French philosopher René Descartes, they believe in doing things by design. They believe not only that there is a 'right' way to teach children, or plan a town, or regulate a bank or grow the economy. They presume that the right way must become *the* way. The right policy must be decided upon and applied for all.

It is this great Cartesian presumption on the part of our elite that pushes us towards ever more statism. It is this that has driven the growth of Big Government, and which explains why over the past century the Western democracies have seen ever more planning, centralisation and top-down government. It accounts for why representative democracy has seen less localised, personalised and individual decision making.

Big Government has grown because public administration is dominated by those who, regardless of what the question might be, believe the answer must always mean a blueprint or a plan – drawn up by people like them.

SOFT BIGOTRY

big·ot ('bɪgət) noun:
One who is strongly partial to one's own group, religion, race, or politics and is intolerant of those who differ.

In almost every Western democracy, the intellectual elite demonstrate a consistent prejudice in favour of deliberately organising economic and social affairs – a Cartesian bias. The would-be designers tend to favour doing things by design.

Conversely, they show a remarkable bigotry against those who favour organising human affairs spontaneously and organically.

Nowhere is this more evident that in the attitudes of the elite towards the free market. Since the elite favour the supposedly disinterested expertise of the elite over the wisdom of the crowd, they are inherently distrustful of the market. The free market is the ultimate bottom-up, spontaneous, organic way of shaping things. No one is in charge. It offends our elite precisely because it makes them redundant.

Amongst the elite, new and unfamiliar ideas are rarely ever assessed on their merits, but in terms of the ease with which 'they fit into general conceptions of what is deemed modern or advanced' ('The Intellectuals and Socialism', F. A. Hayek).

Consider, for example, the attitude of the elite to the idea that the continent of Europe might best be organised by conscious design.

When it comes to a deliberate design, things rarely come along much bigger or grander than the creation of a single European currency for 317 million people in seventeen different countries.

What was the attitude of the elite in Britain and Europe towards it? Biased in favour of Europe by design, bigoted against those who were doubtful.

It is not simply that they overwhelmingly rallied to the cause of a common European currency and made it their own. The elite had little time for – and indeed dismissed as mad – those who argued that Europe might instead benefit from an organic arrangement of competing currencies.

In Whitehall, the Foreign Office and Cabinet Office attempted to persuade successive administrations to keep Britain's option to join open, and to be favourably disposed towards the euro project.

The Confederation of British Industry relentlessly argued in favour of Britain joining the euro.

The motives and integrity of those who questioned

euro membership were regularly called into question. Perfectly rational points about the need for different interest rates were brushed aside, those making them branded racists and xenophobes instead.[36]

Britain's publicly funded broadcaster consistently presented 'the pro-Euro position itself as centre ground, thus defining even moderately Eurosceptic voices as extreme'.[37]

On three consecutive occasions when interviewed by BBC television reporters about the Eurozone crisis, I have had to fend off the interviewers' suggestion that my scepticism about monetary union somehow means that I should want our trading partners to fail. Those of us who believe that Europe is not best organised by some kind of grand Cartesian design have been constantly portrayed as narrow nationalists.

Or take another example. Consider how our elite have responded to the financial crisis since 2007.

You heard them tell us banks were too big to fail, right? In Britain, the BBC's Robert Peston endlessly told us how bailout-and-borrow economics was bold and unavoidable. Indeed, he claimed at length that it was all part of what he termed the 'new capitalism', organised and arranged by design – 'bringing governments together to deal with these risks'.[38]

But can you remember Peston and Co. ever telling us that it might be better if banks were actually allowed to go bust? Ever heard him give serious consideration to the 'no design' option? No public policy of intervention. No attempt to avert the credit crunch by design.

Have you ever heard our publicly funded Business Editor tell us why not bailing out banks would be such a disaster? Or asking if politics can actually solve a financial crisis?

Can you remember the BBC just once interviewing anyone from Iceland, where all the busted banks were allowed to go under, and allowing them to explain that the economy in downtown Reykjavik is actually doing okay? Me neither.

From media expert to public regulator to Treasury minister, since 2007 our elite have presumed that every financial problem could, with enough official fiat, be solved. We have tested that fallacy to destruction without properly considering the alternatives.

In the mind of the elite, state action is always to be favoured over state inaction. Bailouts over letting banks go bust. Corporatism above the free market. Deliberate design over organic constructs.

WHY THE ELITE IS SO OFTEN WRONG

What do urban tower blocks in Britain and Fannie Mae in America have in common? What does European monetary union share with the loose monetary policy in Britain, Japan and America?

They were all, in their different ways, pretty disastrous.

British tower blocks consigned generations of urban Britons to live in monstrous isolation. Fannie Mae sluiced billions of dollars into bad housing loans, almost plunged the world into financial meltdown, cost the US taxpayer hundreds of billions of dollars and forced the US government to increase the national debt by almost $800 billion. The euro has forced millions of Europeans into recession. Years of low interest rates have created a sea of Western debt – and too little saved to maintain living standards.

But these were more than simply bad ideas. They were all disastrous ideas that came *from the top*. They were innovations in housing policy and monetary policy that were conjured up by an elite who, in thrall to various intellectual fads, believed themselves capable of achieving human progress by design. Those responsible for these appalling social and economic policy failures really did regard themselves as the *avant garde*. Yet they led us off a cliff.

Those who, back in 1950s Britain, decided it was time to start housing people in concrete towers had good intentions to improve upon what had gone before. If the British elite built concrete shelves in which to house the masses, the federal authorities in the United States set up Fannie Mae to subsidise their mortgages.

In both cases, the technocrats who designed the policy did so professing to assist the people – but they never did what they did in response to actual popular demand. Fannie Mae was a product of the New Deal 'brains trust'. It subsidised private home ownership precisely because not enough private citizens – thought the experts – wanted home ownership enough to actually buy one without public subsidy.

Tower blocks were the brainchild of elite technocrats like Charles-Édouard Jeanneret. However much we might be told that post-war planners constructed tower blocks on behalf of the people, rarely, if ever, was a tower block built to meet a demand from people prepared to spend their own money to live in one and call it home.

Likewise, European monetary union was the

brainchild of men like Jacques Delors. It was supposed to make the people more prosperous, but it was never introduced by popular demand. In fact, when the people were asked, such as in Sweden in 2003, they voted against it.

Keeping interest rates low in response to just about everything, from the Asian and Russian financial crises of the late 1990s, to the dot com bubble, to September 11, was again an idea that came from the top. It was central bankers like Alan Greenspan who seemed to believe that loose monetary policy was the way to abolish boom and bust forever.

In each case, the genesis of public policy disasters came from above.

But why are the elite so often wrong? How is it that the very people we believe to be a class of disinterested experts able to determine the common interest actually turn out to be wrong?

'Why', asks the brilliant *Economist* writer Janan Ganesh, 'do such clever, experienced people make such bad mistakes?' Noting how disastrously wrong Establishment opinion has been on so many of the great issues of the day, Ganesh raises a profound point. Why have the British elites – who he defines as 'the civil service, the Confederation of British Industry, the universities, the high-brow media, the judiciary, and "fashionable opinion" – been so wrong about so much so often?[39]

Some have looked for answers in behavioural psychology. Others have toyed with the idea that it is all down to the neurological wiring we acquired during our evolutionary past. Apparently, this inclines us to look for patterns and symmetry, causes and effects, even when they are not actually there.[40]

Perhaps. But the answer, Janan, could be much more straightforward. The elite are wrong headed not because there is anything wrong with their neural networks.

The elite get things wrong because they endlessly seek to govern by deliberate design a world that is best organised spontaneously from below. Again and again, public policy failure comes from technocrats and planners who overrate the advantages of deliberate design. They consistently underrate the merits of spontaneous, organic arrangements, and fail to recognise that the best plan is often not to have one.

Think of the elite as being rather like Concorde; top-down technological innovation that publicly funded experts were convinced would transform international air travel. After lots of taxpayer money subsidised the transatlantic travel of a few billionaires and rock stars, it failed.

What most surprises me is not that the elite should be so wrong headed so often, but that anyone should be surprised by it.

Forget about PhDs. The wisdom of the crowd will be superior to that of the elite for the same reason that the free market is better at allocating resources than a committee of planners. Crowd sourcing brings together more knowledge – in all its gloriously fragmented and contradictory form – than a committee of experts can ever possess.

Real knowledge is collective, not individual. You can no more use a select elite to determine the right policy than you can expect them to determine the right price. It simply is not possible to compute all the variables required to enable any elite, no matter how intelligent, to run things well. What is right in one place and at one time may not be so elsewhere. The world is, to use Hayek's phrase, an 'evolutionary rationalist'. It is a place where economic and social affairs are best arranged spontaneously, organically, through a process of trial and error. Where coordination is done on the basis of decentralised, evolutionary design.

The more we come to depend on top-down decision making, the more power we put into the hands of a few individuals. Yet top-down collective decision making denies the crowd the ability to make genuinely collective choices.

We should not be surprised that the elite get so much so wrong. Having the elite decide public policy would be like leaving it to government to design the apps for your iPad. They could do it, but you would probably be waiting a long time and not get quite what you wanted.

The elite are susceptible to intellectual fads, partly because they are because they are so far removed from democratic accountability. This means they are much less likely to ditch daft ideas and assumptions when things start to go wrong.

In Britain, the Foreign and Commonwealth Office decides foreign policy more or less without reference to the elected legislature. This must come as a relief to all those Oxbridge-educated classicists able to get on with the business of statecraft without having to contend with populist pressures.

There are none of those non-experts asking you ill-informed questions about a part of the world they simply do not understand. No one asking why you are cosying up to the Gaddaffi regime in Libya after they blew up a plane over Lockerbie. No one there to wonder, as only a non-Oxbridge thicko might, what would happen to Britain's standing in the Arab world if, having ingratiated ourselves with the tyrants, the Arab people overthrew the despots and dictators. And because no one is asking you those dumb, simplistic questions which only dumb and simplistic non-experts would ever ask, you plough on with a policy that puts you on the wrong side of millions of people throughout the Middle East.

In America, the Federal Reserve Board is virtually immune to public opinion. In fact it was set up that way. Which means that all the sophisticated economics graduates on the board can get on uninterrupted by non-experts.

As JK Galbraith put it, 'in monetary matters as in diplomacy, a nicely conformist nature, a good tailor and the ability to articulate the currently fashionable cliché have usually been better for personal success that an excessively inquiring mind'.[41]

So you leave the well-dressed, agreeable experts to carry on, their Keynesian assumptions intact. Their belief that when in debt, you should spend more unchallenged. Their certainty that you can carry on consuming without producing unquestioned. No dimwitted questions from those without Ivy League degrees asking why, if you are so clever, you got us into such a mess to start with.

Without democratic scrutiny, the difficult questions are seldom asked when they should be. Institutional assumptions go unchallenged within institutions where they become an article of faith. And failure ends up being endlessly reinforced.

Everybody knows the Middle East will never be a democracy, said the expert diplomats. Everybody knows that low interest rates promote economic growth, said the central bankers. Everybody knows government needs to promote wider home ownership, said the politicians.

If the only folk you mix with are the same sort of people who regurgitate the same tepid ideas, picked up from the same secondhand sources that you got them from, perhaps everyone does seem to think like that. But that does not make what you think right.

CHAPTER 4

POLITICS IS DEAD

The delegation of particular technical tasks to separate bodies, while a regular feature, is yet the first step by which a democracy progressively relinquishes its power.
Friedrich Hayek, *The Road to Serfdom*

Politics is dead. As a process for deciding how most Western democracies are governed, politics has come to an end.

Of course elections still happen. Candidates keep running for office. The winners make speeches. But those whom voters elect to office in Britain, America, Japan and Europe no longer decide what government does.

We have reached the stage where government has grown so big, there is simply too much public policy for the public – or their elected representatives – to have much say. A technocratic elite has taken over.

POINTLESS POLITICS
Cast your mind back to the last polling day. Although you certainly had the chance to vote, did you?

Perhaps you were one of the growing numbers of voters across the Western world who seem to have given up voting at all. Participation in British general elections in 2001 fell to its lowest level since the introduction of the universal franchise, when a mere 58 per cent of a voting-age population went to the polling booth. In Britain, one in five people now think that it is 'not really worth voting', compared to just 3 per cent in 1987.[42]

Turnout has been steadily falling in almost every European country, and is lower in America than it was a generation ago.

In French assembly elections, turnout of those of voting age fell from 58 per cent in 1988 to 43 per cent in 2007. It is now normal for most voters in both French assembly elections and US mid-term elections not to vote at all. Reflecting a trend throughout most Western democracies, in Germany the figure fell from 75 per cent in the mid-1980s to 65 per cent in 2009.

But let us assume that you did vote. You are, after all, interested enough to be reading this book. So, what exactly did you think your vote would achieve? Would it determine which school your children went to? Would it put more police on the streets? Would it halt the proposed housing development or determine the site of the incinerator?

Would the person you were voting for lower your taxes, or curb the unaffordable welfare bill you are expected to contribute towards? Did the election determine if government should carry on borrowing billions of pounds your children's children will be expected to pay back? Did it settle the question of how much of our national wealth government should spend? No? Then why did you vote?

Perhaps if you voted you did so out of a sense of civic obligation. Perhaps you are old enough to remember when ballots still had an impact on public policy. After all, here in Britain voters over sixty-five were almost twice as likely to vote at the last general election as those under twenty-five.

It is not that senior citizens are better citizens, but rather that they formed their outlook and attitudes in an age when Parliament was sovereign and when elections still determined the country's future. Older folk vote more often because they formed their outlook in an era before politicians had parcelled out their powers to judges, civil servants, quangos and Eurocrats.

It is not that younger people are filled with apathy. In abstaining, they are behaving entirely rationally. The people standing for office no longer decide, so why bother voting to decide who holds office?

It is not politics that leaves younger voters cold, so much as *elections*. Young people will turn out in large numbers to demonstrate in Wall Street, or rally against trade injustice. But they have accurately clocked that most of the questions they care about are not determined by how they vote. Federal officials decide how to bail out the banks, trade policy is determined by unelected experts.

From the smallest local decision to the largest macro ones, your vote would have settled none of those questions. Indeed, it is precisely because the voters have worked out that their votes count for so little that they have stopped bothering to vote.

As those we elect have lost the power to ameliorate their constituents' circumstances, so they have forfeited their constituents' respect. Ceasing to be authoritative, they have become contemptible.

British voters have become habituated to frustration. Their ballots don't determine where their children can go to school, or whether their local hospital stays open, or where the incinerator is sited, or whether the police patrol their street. Decisions which in other countries are made by local councillors are taken in Britain by unaccountable functionaries.

Turnout at Parliamentary Elections 1987–2012

Percentage of registered voters casting votes, linear trendlines

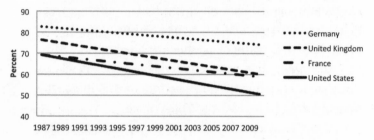

Source: International Institute for Democracy and Electoral Assistance

Elected representatives now have less impact on people's lives than, say, the National Institute for Clinical Excellence, the Highways Agency, the Health and Safety Executive, the Learning and Skills Council or any of a thousand other bodies stretching right up to the European Commission, which, depending on how you measure it, passes between 50 and 80 per cent of our laws. No wonder people don't bother voting.

It is not only in Britain that contempt for the political establishment is running high. In the United States the Tea Party movement is a grass roots insurgency against high-tax-and-spend Washington insiders.

Polls show that a growing number of people agree that politicians are self-interested, know nothing about the real world, make promises they cannot keep, are much of a muchness, don't reflect their views, and will not be able to improve the condition of the country.

Public confidence in MPs in Britain is at an all-time low. Only 26 per cent of people in England think that MPs are dedicated to working well for the public.[43] A mere one in five of the 1,900 people surveyed believed that MPs told the truth.

Even fewer believed that MPs ensured that public money is spent wisely. This contrasts against 93 per cent who trust doctors, according to an earlier survey by the Committee on Standards in Public Life, and 84 per cent who trust head teachers.

A YouGov poll in the *Daily Telegraph* in February 2008 showed that only 4 per cent of people believe that MPs put the country before themselves, and an astonishing 79 per cent agree with the statement 'most MPs use public office to make money improperly'.

While a measure of cynicism towards the political class is a feature of most democracies, the current level of distrust is unprecedented – and has not in any way abated with a change of government.

There is, according to Peter Kellner of YouGov, 'a massive discontent that goes far beyond a dislike of particular politicians, parties and policies'. YouGov's political attitudes survey[44] undertaken in 2012 found that the majority in Britain 'believe [the political system] to be fundamentally flawed'. A mere 15 per cent of people felt their own MP was 'doing a good job'. Sixty-two per cent agreed with the statement that 'politicians tell lies all the time – you cannot believe a word they say'. Almost 60 per cent were of the view that it made no difference as to which political party wins elections.

The tide of anti-politics sentiment in the West is not only reflected in falling turnout. It can be measured by falling membership of political parties. In almost every country in western Europe, membership of political parties fell between 2002/03 and 2008/09. In Spain and Portugal, membership of a political party almost halved. The only two countries where party membership increased during that time were the Netherlands and Denmark, where radically anti-Establishment, anti-politician parties competed for market share with the established mainstream political parties.[45]

PARASITICAL POLITICIANS

Fifth-century France was ruled by a dynasty of Merovingian kings. Once a force to be feared, successive Merovingian monarchs parcelled power out to courtiers – where it remained.

Gradually the retainers took over. By the sixth century, the Merovingians had become ceremonial figureheads. Their presence on the throne lent legitimacy to decisions made by others who sat behind it.

In our own time something similar has happened to those we elect to office.

Power from elected officials has been parcelled out to the unelected. Civil servants and technocrats make more and more of the decisions. Democratically elected ministers might remain the source of authority. Their presence in the department, or signature on the document, might still be necessary to give it legitimacy. But it is increasingly the courtiers, not those we elect, who govern over us.

Elected politicians resemble Merovingian weaklings in other ways, too.

Despised for their weakness, the Merovingians became known as the *rois fainéants* – or the 'do-nothing kings'.

Parasitical do-nothings.

It sounds like a pretty good description of how many people might talk about elected politicians today.

Eventually, in 752, the last Merovingian weakling – Childeric – was packed off to die in a monastery. Might the same thing happen to those we elect? Might they, too, be bundled out of the way and power pass entirely to the technocratic elite? It seems to have happened in Italy and Greece already, where unelected Euro officials packed off two elected Prime Ministers.

We have reached the stage where, in a reversal of 200 years of political thinking, the mere fact of having been elected to office is seen as a disqualification.

This is, on the face of it, a curious finding. You would think that someone who depends on our votes would be thought of as less remote, more accountable, than someone who doesn't. But here we reach the crux. People no longer regard the electoral process as anything to do with them. They see politicians as a separate caste.

In Britain, the Electoral Commission embarked on a major qualitative study to explain the electorate's attitude towards those they voted for. The findings of its focus groups were, in the curious way that these things sometimes are, both predictable and shocking. People felt wholly disconnected from their politicians. They spoke of them almost as one would speak of an occupying power. To quote from the Electoral Commission's summary:

> People do not regard politicians as their representatives, the champions of their interests, but as a privileged and distant elite, in their own world and with next

to no understanding of the lives of ordinary people. The catch-all use of 'they' is applied indiscriminately.

This language seems more fitted to a dictatorship than a democracy. Think how aptly the above paragraph would apply to, say, the *apparatchiks* of the Soviet bloc. They, too, were thought to inhabit their own world. The country they described in their official propaganda – one with soaring production, full quotas and regular elections – bore no relation to that which their subjects could see around them. The attitude of voters towards politics in contemporary Britain is disquietingly similar to that of the captive peoples of the Comecon states: sullen, cynical, fatalistic.

How can this be when politicians are obliged repeatedly to reapply for their jobs through open elections?

The answer is staring us in the face. The politician is no longer able to discharge his primary function. He cannot effect meaningful change in his constituents' lives. He has therefore ceased to be a vessel for popular will.

No longer an agent of change, he has become a parasite.

VIRTUAL GOVERNMENT

'They pretend to pay us and we pretend to work' ran the old joke in the Soviet Union.

In our defunct Western democracy one might perhaps say that the politicians pretend to govern us and we pretend to vote for them.

But the reality is that those we elect to high office do not make many of the key public policy decisions that affect our lives.

Why not? Why can't those we vote into office change things? Why doesn't government respond to the will of the governed?

When you make a decision that only concerns you – where to shop or where to go on holiday – you and the family decide. Then off you go.

But as soon as you start making choices on behalf of a few more people, things get more tricky.

Think back to the last time someone at the office suggested you all get together after work. Perhaps there was an endless exchange of emails. Tom suggested meeting up on Thursday evening at Nando's, while Dick preferred Pizza Express. Harry, meanwhile, wanted to know why we couldn't all make it on Friday instead.

A group does not have to get very big before genuinely collective decision making can become hard. You soon find that the decisions get passed over to one or two people to make – 'Dick went ahead and booked a table at Pizza Express. Let him know if you can make it.'

The trouble is that that is pretty much how many of our public policy choices end up having to be made, too. Decisions are delegated to a few – and not everyone is satisfied. That might be fine if you are choosing where to eat a pizza. But putting up with what Dick has decided for you is less easily done when it involves the most expensive purchasing decisions you are likely to make in your life.

If we contract out decision making to a few Dicks, we soon discover that the only thing collective about their choices is the way the rest of us have to go along with them. Top-down collective choices usually end up with the collective having little say. And the more public policy there is in society, the less choice the actual public tends to get.

Western democracies have some enormously complex health plans, social security programmes and education systems. Through them, choices that will affect the lives of millions of people are made. But in practice, it often really boils down to having the decision made by Dick.

In fact, when it comes to public service provision, we do not just leave it to Dick to decide on the restaurant. We do the equivalent of leaving it to him to select the menu for us. Tom, Harry and the rest of us rely on schools and hospitals that Dick runs for us, and have to accept what he has chosen.

If you would rather not leave it to someone at work to order a £10 pizza for you, why are you prepared to have someone select what kind of public services you get when you are spending the lion's share of your earnings paying for it?

'But we all get a vote to decide,' I hear you say. 'Top-down collective decisions might apply to millions of voters, but millions of voters have a choice when they elect someone to office.'

Hummmm. Nice theory, but where do you see that happening in practice?

When you vote to elect a candidate for public office, you are voting to elect a candidate to office. You are not voting to decide what is on the menu.

A binary decision between Republican or Democrat, Conservative or Labour, Gaullist or Socialist is not a choice as to what is on the menu. It is not even a choice as to who decides what is on the menu. It is a choice between someone offering to supervise the person making

those choices for you one way, and someone else offering to supervise a little differently.

The best-case scenario is that the person you vote in
might encourage the person doing the deciding to hand
you a selection a little more to your liking than what
the other guy might do.

It is not even as if the politicians you vote for make
most of the choices. They have abdicated responsibility over a range of issues.

A bewildering and costly range of quangos and
federal agencies – unelected bodies unaccountable to
anyone you voted for – have taken control of many of the
functions of government. Across Europe, much of our
legislation is now made not by elected parliamentarians, but in Brussels. Federal officials in the US and
the EU, not ministers, make decisions within the civil
service. Central bankers set interest rates and print
more money.

Even where laws are still passed by Congress or
Parliament, they are reinterpreted according to the
whim of activist judges. In Britain, judges use human
right rules to determine school uniform codes. In
America, judges decide the law on gay marriage
in California despite, rather than because of, what
the voters want.

The bigger government gets, the more those we
elect abdicate decision making. With over a thousand
quangos in Britain, and a mere 650 MPs, it is simply
not possible for those we elect to keep track of all the
things that all that extra government is doing, let alone
take responsibility directly for all the choices that
they make.

Having gone to the trouble of getting myself elected

to Parliament, I saw this problem almost immediately I set foot in the House of Commons. Concerned that some of my constituents in the early stages of Alzheimer's disease were not being offered a full range of treatment, I asked to meet the health minister to discuss it.

A charming woman, she expressed genuine concern. But the problem, she told me, was that it was not her, or me, or anyone else the public elected, that decided these things. Britain's National Health Service might be there to provide health care to the public, but the people the public vote for at election time do not appear to run it. A government agency called the National Institute for Clinical Excellence – or NICE – gets to decide which patients get the treatment.

The best that any elected MP could do, she cheerfully told me, was to lobby all the Dicks who work there and hope they change their mind. In fact, most weeks the majority of letters that I write as a Member of Parliament are addressed to various officials in an effort to lobby them on behalf of my electorate.

It does not matter who you vote for, the same remote officials remain in charge.

But how can you vote NICE out of office? You can't.

And they don't just arbitrate our access to health care. They preside over whole tranches of public policy that have been lifted out of the democratic process.

Not even those elected ministers are able to hold the alphabet soup of officialdom to account.

Even when they want to make changes, they find that they simply cannot decree it. Encased in bureaucracy, they tug at levers only to find that they are loose, and jab at buttons that have long since been disconnected from the machine they purport to drive. Pledges given in good faith cannot be fulfilled: the machinery of state had become too inert to respond.

This might make voters cynical, but in my experience it makes politicians cynical, too.

Once ministers realise that they cannot effect meaningful change, they try instead to show that they are active. The criminal justice system's deep-seated failings cannot be remedied, so the minister makes a trite announcement about forcing offenders to work. The immigration system is enormously complex and difficult to sort out, so the minister issues a press release suggesting benefits claimants must learn English.

In Britain, laws have become increasingly declamatory, intended to 'send a message' rather than remedy a problem; the Dangerous Dogs Act, the Football Spectators Act, the EU Referendum 'lock'.

Ministers send out blizzards of press releases announcing Initiatives and Zones and Action Plans and New Deals. Instead of having a clear list of actions that need to be done, ministers have a 'media grid' indicating which announcements will be made when. Press officers have become more important than policy wonks. Presentation more important than substance.

In the absence of real power, appearance is all.

Thus has our system of democratic politics been hollowed out from within. It has become a husk. It retains its outward shape and form. But the substance and meaning has withered and shrunk.

CHAPTER 5

STATES OF INCOMPETENCE

It is so easy to be fooled when you want to believe.
Ferdinand Mount

Here is a list of news stories, picked out at random from Western news sources in recent months:

- One in five British adults remain 'functionally illiterate' having passed through school without having learnt to read and write properly – *The Sun, April 16 2012*.
- Six million Britons were billed the wrong amount of tax because of a calculation error by Her Majesty's Revenue and Customs – *BBC online, September 4 2011*.
- Two US naval ships, which cost $300 million, are to be scrapped despite never leaving dock on a mission in the twenty five years it took to build them – *The Virginian-Pilot, July 15 2011*.
- Not a single Royal Navy warship was available to defend the British coastline last month, despite Britain having the fifth largest defence budget in the world – *Daily Telegraph, November 2 2011*.

- UK Border Agency staff routinely failed to check the passports of those trying to enter the country – *The Guardian, November 7 2011.*
- Passengers at London's Heathrow are 'regularly queuing for up to two hours to pass through immigration' – *The Economist online, April 30 2012.*
- Radical Islamic preacher Sheikh Raed Salah was able to stroll past UK Border Agency officials and enter Britain – despite having been officially banned from entering – *BBC online, June 29 2011.*
- The European Commission provided €35 million to get 9,000 long term unemployed construction workers back to work. Two years after the money was awarded, none of the unemployed workers due to be retrained had even been contacted about the scheme – *Irish Industry News, November 21 2011.*
- Four patients die each day in British NHS hospitals from thirst or malnutrition – *Daily Mail, January 22 2012.*
- Germany's intelligence services lost the blueprints for its new €1.6 billion agency headquarters – *BBC online, July 11 2011.*
- Thousands of people in Britain have been wrongly branded criminals by the Criminal Records Bureau – *Daily Mail, April 14 2010.*

Western governments, it seems, often struggle to carry out their basic functions. Why is this?

Partly it is because they are just too big.

But the disadvantages of being big – poor communication, inflexibility – are not the only problem. It is partly due to the fact that officialdom is simply unaccountable.

Big government + little accountability = disastrous public policy.

Officials often administer policies on the basis of certain presumptions and unproven theories, which they have elevated to the status of inviolable fact. With little scrutiny and lots of self-interest, public administrators often fail to recognise that their approach is wrong headed. Failure is not just more likely, but tends to get reinforced.

BIG IS CLUMSY

> To the size of a state there is a limit, as there is to plants, animals and implements, for they can none of them retain their facility when they are too large.
> Aristotle

The larger an organisation, the more hierarchical it tends to be – and therefore the less responsive and adaptive it becomes. It is not only ancient Greek philosophers that understood this. In recent years the observation has dominated business management.

Influential books such as *The Myth of Leadership* by Jeffrey Nielsen and *The End of Management* by Kenneth Cloke and Joan Goldsmith have pointed out how large hierarchical organisations tend to mean that information is monopolised, decision making is tightly controlled and communication becomes unreliable.

Big organisations become inefficient because of communication failure. Subordinates are often reluctant to present the full picture to their line managers, sometimes not wanting to pester their superiors, sometimes wanting to look as if they are able to handle things, sometimes simply being reluctant to be the bearers of bad news. In consequence, line managers can have a *less* complete picture of what is happening than those beneath them. And those at the very top can be the most cut off of all.

Precisely because of this, for the past twenty or thirty years there has been some pretty major restructuring of the typical Western business model. Layers of management and hierarchy have gone. Offices have gone 'open plan' to encourage interaction. Great efforts have been put into encouraging more effective feedback and communication.

The typical Western business model is a lot less top down and hierarchical. But the model for government remains largely unchanged.

While the chief executive of Tesco now likes to boast that no more than six levels of hierarchy separate him from the check-out girl, government ministries remain wholly unreconstructed. How many levels of hierarchy separate the minister for education from the classroom assistant?

As Kenneth Boulding puts it, 'the larger and more authoritarian the organisation, the better the chance that its top decision-makers will be operating in purely imaginary worlds'. The sheer size of public administration means that many of the top public policy makers are making decisions within imaginary worlds.

Consider, for example, the research into 'cognitive biases' inspired by Daniel Kahneman and Amos Tversky. Kahneman and Tversky made the discovery that experts are prone to particular kinds of errors of judgement: the sunk-costs phenomenon, egocentric distortions, the bandwagon effect and so on.

For example, fund managers tend, on average, to underperform the stock exchange. Having worked in fund management, it hurts me to write this, but most of us would be better off buying shares at random than asking a professional to do it for us. If professional money men are surprisingly bad at handling our affairs, logic suggests that the same is even truer of the civil servants and ministers who lack the fund managers' incentives.

Or consider 'transactions-cost economics', inspired by the Nobel Prize-winning economist Ronald Coase and developed by Oliver Williamson.

Williamson's interest was in comparing the costs of running something internally with those of the external market. Amongst other things, he found that the larger an organisation becomes, and the more it takes on, the less efficient it becomes. Most management consultants know this, of course; but the logic is rarely extended to government departments.

Big government is difficult to manage precisely because it is so big. To make matters worse, those in charge of public administration often get things wrong because they tend to implement policy on the basis of knowledge and theories that are presumed to be true – but which often turn out to be false.

PUBLIC POLICY DOGMA

dogma ('dɒgmə)
An authoritative principle, belief, or statement of ideas or opinion, especially one considered to be absolutely true.

Western leaders like to imply that they are pragmatic, interested in doing 'what works'. In reality, however, the technocratic elite who determine policy turn out to be remarkably dogmatic.

If you stop to think about it, claiming to know 'what works' is remarkably presumptuous. It implies that you know how things work – that you are in possession of some absolute truths. Confident of their ability to organise society in accordance with their conception of 'what works', public officials presuming to have absolute truths often turn out to have only theories. And theories, it turns out, are often informed as much by fashionable ideas as by fact.

Technocrats often stick with the theory long after empirical evidence showing that it was flawed would convince a true pragmatist – with less confidence in the power of grand designs – to try a different approach.

Far from working, elitist design often turns out to be conceit. It produces not progress, let alone utopia, but Western economic decline, social decay and fiscal crisis. Failure is reinforced and rewarded. Perverse incentives encourage people to do the wrong thing. Innovation is stifled.

Worse, dogma means that the governing classes in the West – the politicians, civil servants, technocrats, academics and officials – have the wrong priorities. Unproven theories see them claiming that they have the ability to change the climate and the level of the oceans. But they cannot even enforce basic border controls. Thanks to dogma, they have come to see the former as vital – yet they do not seem to bother much with the basics of statecraft.

The result has been a cumulative – and ultimately catastrophic – system of maladministration, with

Western states now lurching from one crisis to another. We have been brought low by the grand delusions of unaccountable technocrats. The grander their designs and ambitions, and the greater their faith in false premise, the bigger disaster public policy has been.

MICRO DOGMA: BROOKLANDS – THE POOREST PLACE IN ENGLAND

Ayn Rand's dystopian novel, *Atlas Shrugged*, describes the fictional American town of Starnesville. A once prosperous community housing employees of the Twentieth Century Motor Company, Starnesville has been reduced to ruin: 'The empty structures were vertical rubble ... Boards torn out at random, missing patches of roofs ... the inhabited houses were scattered at random among the ruins.'

Rand's Starnesville might be fictional, but Brooklands in my English constituency is not. Yet it, too, is a town where 'the houses stand like men in unpressed suits'. Brooklands, too, was built for car workers – not working for an imaginary Twentieth Century Motor Company, but for the real one, Ford.

But you will struggle to find anything industrious about Brooklands today. The poorest place in England, 62 per cent of working-age adults live on benefits. There is someone on welfare in almost every home. A person living in Brooklands is three times as likely as the average Brit to suffer from heart disease or chronic illness.

Why? How could a once thriving community become so poor?

Mixed between dilapidated houses stand empty plots of land, overrun by brambles and old mattresses. I once spent a weekend helping pull abandoned washing machines and rusting junk from the scrubland. They sprouted back with surprising vigour over the weeks that followed.

What happened to the pride? How is it that a neighbourhood could end up in a state of grim despair?

In Rand's novel, Starnesville illustrates what happens when wealth creators are driven out. Real-life Brooklands shows what can happen when remote officials make public policy without having to answer to the public.

You see, Brooklands is at risk of flooding. Parts of it lie below sea level.

It is not topography that has proved to be the problem, but officialdom.

'A risk of flooding!' thought the officials at the Environment Agency. 'We'd better not let folk build there then.'

So a 'no build / no planning permission' policy has been in force – in everything but name – for years. It has had appalling consequences.

To be sure, Brooklands *is* at risk of floods. But how does a ban on building anything make local people more safe from flood waters? How has consigning a generation of local people to live in single-storey wooden houses made them less in danger of being inundated by the sea?

Across the other side of the North Sea, around a third of Holland lies below mean sea level. If Dutch authorities had applied the same 'logic' as the UK's Environment Agency, there would have been no new homes built in much of the Netherlands since 1970-something.

Many of the building applications that officials have been merrily turning down for Brooklands have been for precisely the kind of two-storey houses that would make local people less at risk. Yet separated by all those layers of hierarchy, it does not seem to have occurred to officials that rather than protecting local people, a 'no build' policy has merely ensured that more local people are at greater risk should there be a flood.

It does not seem to have occurred to them that as a consequence of their policy, there has been almost zero private investment in the housing stock in Brooklands for decades. With no home improvements, people have been unable to improve the quality of their homes and the housing stock has deteriorated.

With no prospect of being able to build new homes, owners have been forced to watch as their simple, single-storey bungalows fall apart. With the value of the housing stock falling, there have been few buyers. Those who did choose to buy were often desperate and, once they had bought, found themselves trapped.

To be fair, the blanket ban on planning has not been entirely responsible for the dilapidated state of the neighbourhood. Once the downward spiral started, many individual owners sold up to landlords who had discovered that they could make money offering substandard accommodation to desperate tenants on welfare.

But if the official ban on development is not the only explanation for the state of Brooklands, it goes a long way to explaining why Brooklands looks like Brooklands and not like the neighbourhood where you live.

Of course the Environment Agency would deny that any of this is the intention of their policy. But then who would have thought that an agency set up to oversee environmental protection would end up deciding housing policy?

That is what happens when you leave it to remote officials to make policy on the basis of what they know to be

right for other people – without these people being able
to hold officials to account. Organisations established to
do one thing end up doing other things. Advice acquires
the force of law. And what the 'experts' decide, no matter
how absurd the dogma, is what happens.

Dogma on the part of public officials in England has
left several hundred people living in substandard housing. Dogma on the other side of the Atlantic designed to
get people out of substandard housing almost crashed
the world economy.

MACRO DOGMA: THE US SUBPRIME BUBBLE

Rarely do public policy catastrophes come along on
quite the titanic scale of the US subprime housing
bubble. This is perhaps fortunate, given that it almost
sank the entire Western banking system.

After rising rapidly from the mid-1990s, US house
prices peaked in 2006. They then started to fall
dramatically. The Case-Schiller price index recorded
its largest fall ever between 2007 and 2011, with house
prices 30 per cent below their peak. Between 2006 and
2011, 1.2 million Americans lost their homes.

This dramatic increase in foreclosures by home
owners unable to keep up mortgage payments meant
misery for millions. It also triggered a subprime crisis,
sparking the global credit crunch.

'But it was the markets, not public policy, that caused
the crash,' I hear you say.

True. The markets caused the housing bubble to
burst. But they did so only in the sense that they called
time on a bubble that public officials had inflated in the
first place. Blaming markets for bringing the US housing bubble down to earth is like blaming gravity when

an aeroplane crashes. It makes more sense to examine what went wrong when things were sent skyward.

The soaring US housing market that preceded the crash was a direct consequence of public policy decisions made by unaccountable officials within the alphabet soup of government: by the Department of Housing and Urban Development, known as HUD, and the Federal National Mortgage Association, known as Fannie Mae, to be specific.

Determined to increase home ownership amongst the poor, and particularly amongst minority groups, HUD embarked on an aggressive drive to try to use the law to force mortgage lenders to lend more readily to 'disadvantaged' groups.

Law suits were brought against banks and mortgage companies. HUD officials monitored lenders for signs of 'disparate treatment', and hauled some through the courts for not lending enough. In 1996, HUD was able to set legally binding targets for Fannie Mae: 42 per cent of their lending had to be to borrowers with incomes below the median income in their area. In 2005, the target rose to 52 per cent. HUD even set a target that decreed one in four loans made by Fannie Mae had to be extended to people with very low incomes. HUD actively encouraged mortgages with only 3 per cent deposit requirements.

Subprime loans were not a product of the free market. They were federal policy.

Banks were forced to make loans to people who could not afford them – and to whom the banks would not otherwise have lent. 'The Federal Reserve Bank of Boston published a manual for lenders ... which advised them that a mortgage applicant's lack of credit history should not be seen as a negative factor in assessing them for a loan; that lenders should not flinch if borrowers used loans for their mortgage deposit; and that unemployment benefits would be a valid source of income for lending decisions. It also reminded them that failing to meet [federal] regulations could be a violation of the law and might expose them to actual damages plus punitive damages of $500,000'.[46]

The officials got their way. Their grand design worked. For a while.

Between 1995 and 2004, an extra 4.6 million Americans became home owners. More than two million black and Hispanic Americans were able to buy homes for the first time. Not only were there more home owners, but the value of their assets rose sharply. With a roaring property market, it seemed for a while as if simply owning a home would pay for itself.

But then the grand design started to go wrong. Once house prices stopped rising and the cost of a loan went up, suddenly mortgage debt no longer paid for itself. All those subprime lenders started to miss their payments.

Banks that had merrily bought debts from Fannie Mae in the expectation that someone somewhere was going to be servicing them began to realise it wasn't so. Worse, with falling house prices, the assets against which all those loans had been secured were worth a lot less than they thought. Banks far removed from the US housing market were suddenly revealed to have vast gaps in their balance sheets where all those subprime loans were. Banks in America, Europe and around the world had to be rescued by governments – or allowed to go bust.

Fannie Mae went bust and had to call upon the federal government to step in to guarantee $789 billion worth of loans. It is estimated that the cost to the taxpayer of bailing out Fannie Mae could be between $224 and $360 billion in total, with over $150 billion already lost. The federal authorities have acknowledged losing $400 billion in trying to deal with the collapsing housing bubble – and several years on it is far from certain that the collapse is over.

What is so striking about this epic disaster, however, is the way that the policy of publicly subsidised mortgage provision came about. It happened with almost zero public accountability. Far from HUD and Fannie Mae responding to democratic pressure via Congress, it was the other way round. Fannie actively lobbied Congress, engaged in politics and directly funded legislators' election campaigns. It was the unelected driving the elected, not the unelected responding to the elected.

Under both Democrats and Republicans, politicians of all parties seemed content to simply recycle a script written for them by federal officials.

What is more, the policy was financed without the need to get Congressional approval. Since 1968, Fannie Mae's accounts no longer appeared on the US Treasury balance sheet. Fannie Mae – and HUD – were thus able to sluice billions of dollars into a policy of mortgage subsidy with only the most cursory democratic oversight.

The experts at HUD and at Fannie Mae did not get things wrong because they were bad people. Actually, I think they were trying to extend home ownership for the noblest of reasons. But they did so with disastrous consequences for the simple reason that their theorising got things the wrong way round. They mistook cause and effect.

Since communities in America with high levels

of home ownership tended to have lower crime and higher levels of employment and educational attainment, HUD's experts presumed that the former was the cause of the latter.

Federal housing experts seemed unable or unwilling to consider that less poverty, higher employment and lower crime in a community might explain why more people owned their own home, rather than the other way round. Thus did they sluice billions of dollars into a policy that has pushed millions of poor Americans into taking on debts that they can never repay.

Post hoc, ergo propter hoc. Because one thing follows another, it is presumed to be its effect.

The experts at the Environment Agency also got things the wrong way round. They correctly recognised the high risk of flooding. But they wrongly presumed that the best way to protect local people is to discourage new building, when they could instead have permitted people to build newer, more flood-resistant buildings.

Sometimes big government does not merely get things the wrong way round. Often the entire theory on which policy is based is flawed – to everyone apart from the experts.

A WELFARE STATE OF DOGMA: PUBLIC SERVICES IN BRITAIN

Everybody knows that government has to provide public services. Why? Because, as everyone also knows, public services are better provided by government that they would be if we were each left to obtain those services for ourselves. And because every right-thinking person knows this to be so, it must be. Right?

This has certainly been the prevalent view in Britain and Europe for most of the past sixty years. It is on this basis that Britain's welfare state was established. It is in the knowledge that government provides best that there have been sixty two Health Acts, fifty four Social Security Acts and forty four Education Acts.

It is not just laws that have been enacted on this principle. Billions of pounds have been spent in the certainty that government does public services best. So certain do we seem to be of the principle that since 2000, we have doubled public spending on health, education and social security.

Public spending since 1940 at constant prices

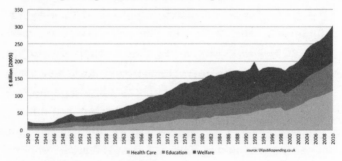

Source: ukpublicspending.co.uk

But the belief that government is better able to provide public services is exactly that – a belief, an article of faith. At times, perhaps, almost a religious conviction. But is it a belief that can be maintained once it has come into contact with the facts?

For sure, some public services – by their very nature – can only be provided for everyone, or not at all. Either we have an army, navy and air force protecting the whole country, or we do not. You could not ask the armed forces to only look out for certain bits of the nation.

But why is it preferable that government should collectively provide us with, say, health care or education?

I can sense your growing outrage. 'Health and education are vital!' you cry. 'Government must provide them.'

The food we eat is pretty vital, too. Without it we would starve. Yet I do not see government-run farms, or supermarkets, or restaurants the way I do state-run schools and hospitals. Just because something is important to us, why does it follow that officialdom must take responsibility? Are officials really better at deciding things for us than we are at deciding for ourselves?

'Yes. That's it,' you retort, scrambling to think of a reason to justify what everybody knows. 'We need government to run these things because that way we get better provision.'

Let's take a quick look at the evidence for this government-provides-it-better thesis.

In Britain, government spends over £90 billion a year providing over 90 per cent of children with an education. What sort of head start in life do young people get from it?

Of course, there are many examples of excellence in the state sector. With over 90 per cent of children in it, there would have to be. But at the same time, there are some shocking facts about the state-run system, too.

A third of children leave primary school unable to read and write.[47] In London, one in five leave second-ary school unable to read or write properly.[48] Sixteen per cent of British adults have the literacy skills below those expected of an eleven-year year old.[49]

It is not just that the state-provided system of education is not good enough in objective terms. The system of education run by government is indisputably behind the independent education system that government does not run – and it is falling behind further each year.

With the amount of money spent on the state education sector almost doubling over the past decade, we have tested to destruction the idea that standards are all down to money. Government is just not very good at running schools.

Independent schools overall perform better than state schools. Within the state sector, church schools tend to do better than non-church schools. Academies, which have autonomy, generally achieve higher grades than schools run by local government. The further away from government a school is, the better it tends to be.

Far from being better at providing education for us, all the evidence points the other way; government is actually worse at providing education for us than the non-government sector.

What about the idea that government-run health care is better health care?

In Britain, the government-run system of health care has an almost 100 per cent monopoly. Over the past ten years, spending on it has rocketed by 70 per cent, from £60 billion to £102 billion. How is it performing compared to those non-government systems around the world?

The government-run health system in Britain

has significantly higher mortality rates compared to the mixed system across the Channel in continental Europe. Indeed, 11,749 more people die under Britain's *dirigiste* system of health care than would die if they were being cared in a mixed European system.[50] By many measures, such as cancer survival rates, Britain's health system fails to perform as well as the health care systems in Singapore and the United States, too. Far from a better system of health care, a government-run monopoly is demonstrably worse.

The dogma is demonstrably wrong. Government-run education is not as good as the education system provided by the non-government sector. Britain's system of government-provided health care has worse outcomes than comparable mixed-provision systems.

'But it is about equality, too,' you insist. 'We need government to run things to make sure society is fair.'

Fair, you say?

In 2011, spot checks in Britain's hundred leading hospitals found that most older people were not being fed properly and were routinely malnourished; 'elderly patients were left rattling their bed rails or hitting water jugs on tables to attract nurses' attention'.[51] They seemed to have a fair chance of being ignored.

According to other reports, four patients die malnourished and thirsty in NHS hospitals each day.[52] Yet another discovered how older patients are routinely left to go hungry, unwashed or given the wrong medication because of the 'casual indifference of staff'.[53]

Perhaps by equality, you mean that older patients seem to have an equal chance of being left lying in their own filth? In November 2011, the Patients Association documented systematic neglect on hospital wards with a dying woman's family having to beg for painkillers for two hours and older patients left to sit in their own faeces and going without food and drink.[54] It has not been unheard of for patients in NHS hospitals to die of thirst because no one bothered to give them anything to drink.[55]

'But you are just cherry-picking some extreme examples and anecdotes,' comes your response.

Okay, so let us measure NHS performance in aggregate and mathematically.

For the past decade, spending on the NHS has increased by 4.6 per cent each year. Yet the productivity of the service has actually fallen by 0.2 per cent a year, with productivity in hospitals falling by 1.4 per cent.

Brits increased the amount they spent on the government-knows-best-for-me approach by 54 per cent between 1997 and 2007. Yet they got a mere 24 per cent increase in services.[56]

As an individual consumer, imagine you went to a supermarket and spent £154 where previously you had only ever spent £100. How might you feel if when you checked your shopping trolley on the way out, you discovered that far from getting an extra £54 worth of groceries for that extra £54 you had had to pay, you had only got £24 worth of extra shopping?

You would feel ripped off. Yet that is precisely what the leave-it-to-government-to-do-it-for-you approach has done for us all. How can such a system possibly be regarded as fair?

Everybody knows that government has to provide health care, apparently. Yet because government is providing it for everyone, we never quite get to see what a bad deal we each get out of it as individuals.

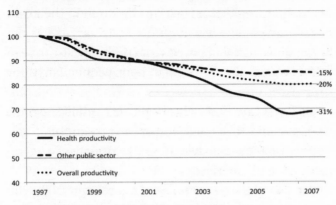

Declining public sector productivity in England

Source: Tullett Prebon, *Thinking the Unthinkable.*

'But it is not just about us as individuals, but social justice' comes your last-gasp defence of the idea that government is better at doing things for us. 'For the common good, government has to do all these things to reduce poverty and income inequality.'

In the belief that government can reduce poverty and inequality, Britain now spends an extraordinary 25 per cent of national income on social protection benefits.[57] Over the past ten years, the social security budget has doubled from £60 billion a year to £111 billion today. We now hand out more in welfare cheques every year than the entire national income of Bangladesh, a country of 150 million people.

But where is the evidence that it has achieved what it was supposed to? Has it actually lifted former recipients out of poverty? Have any of those social security budgets withered away, victims of their own success?

The opposite has happened.

There are now 4.9 million people in Britain living

on benefit[58] – approximately 13 per cent of the adult population, and in some parts of the country the figure rises to almost one in five adults.

Far from reducing poverty, paying people to be poor has increased the numbers of poor people. Forty per cent of Britons now receive some kind of state hand-out.[59] Twelve million UK households contain someone who is receiving welfare. One in five British children is raised in a home in which no adult works.[60]

As we have doubled welfare spending since 1998, we have doubled the number of households in Britain where no one has ever worked.[61] Despite real incomes amongst the bottom decile in Britain doubling over the past half-century, spending to alleviate poverty is vastly higher than it was back then.[62]

For every ten people in employment in Britain, there is one person living at their expense on inca-pacity benefit claiming to be unable to work – despite a recent pilot study finding that three out of four claimants medically examined either withdrew their application or were proved to be capable of working.[63]

The common good, you said? What is good about the fact that 900,000 people in Britain have been living on 'sickness benefit' for over a decade?[64]

Social justice, you said? What is just about having more than 100,000 British households receiving more in net benefits every year than the average working Briton earns?[65]

Everybody knows that government has to provide social security. Yet does everyone also believe that social security payments are really about provid-ing a social security 'safety net'? Is it not obvious that social security has become a regular source of income across many income groups?

Everyone knows that it is better to have government run the health system for us. Then as an individual parent of a sick two-year-old you try to find a GP on a Saturday afternoon.

Does everyone get told to call back for an appointment next Tuesday? Does everyone normally have to sit for four hours with a screaming toddler in A&E, surrounded by drunks?

As you make your way home in the small hours of the morning, dropping into a 24-hour Tesco to get the kid some breakfast, you wonder how the supermarkets manage to be open when you need them. So why not the GP?

Everyone knows that government is better at providing education. But then you start to wonder what it would be like if the government were to run supermarkets like they run schools. Might there be catchment areas for breakfast cereals and waiting lists for vegetables? So you stop thinking about it, and go back to what everyone knows to be right.

That's the thing with dogma. It often trumps the empirical evidence around us. Like blind adherence to any faith, it can leave people believing in contradictory things, unwilling to let reason get in the way of their devotion. Those who point this out run the risk of being treated as heretics.

DOGMA ON AN INTERNATIONAL SCALE: WESTERN AID POLICY

Rich Western countries ought to help poorer nations in Africa and the less developed world. I hope you agree.

When famine or natural disaster strikes, it is only right to send aid and relief. But it is not simply a case of helping out during an emergency. We should want to help everyone achieve prosperity.

Philanthropy is not dogma, but decency.

Wanting to help other people less fortunate than ourselves might be the right thing to want to do, but do we do it right?

There has certainly been no lack of Western aid effort. Setting aside emergency famine and disaster relief, over the past sixty years Western governments have devoted an enormous $2 trillion of official development assistance, or ODA, to try to help less developed countries develop, mostly in Africa.

To put the scale of that effort in to context, $2 trillion totals approximately three times the size of the South African economy, Africa's largest. Or about the size of sub-Saharan Africa's GDP.[66]

How has the West spent $2 trillion worth of assistance helping Africa and the less developed world? Being development assistance, it has not gone on food rations. Nor has it been spent on, say, $2 trillion worth of tariff reductions. Instead, Western aid has been largely about capital transfers in one form or another.

From micro finance projects to large infrastructure programmes, the West has spent about $2 trillion over six decades injecting capital into the economies of less developed countries.

Why channel aid to Africa this way? Because as every aid expert over the past few decades knows, Africa is poor because she lacks capital.

According to 'investment gap theory', underdeveloped economies are underdeveloped because they lack enough capital to enable them to diversify. Without capital to invest in growth, undercapitalised countries have remained poor. Inject capital, and they will take off.

There is one problem with this certainty, upon which Western aid policy rests: it is not true.

Studies looking at the relationship between per capita overseas development assistance and changes in GDP show that there is no correlation. None. Zilch. Hakuna in any language.

According to Rajan & Subramanian[67] there is no evidence of any link between aid inflows into a country and economic growth. No net effect on growth. We have spent $2 trillion on a false premise, a dogma that turns out to be false.

Not only have we spent money buying development that does not work, we are gearing up to throw even greater sums on a false premise. In 2009, the UK government increased development aid spending to £7.4 billion, with a promise to increase it to 0.7 per cent of GDP.

By any objective assessment, Western development spending has failed to achieve development. It may even be retarding it.

As the Zambian-born economist Dambisa Moyo suggested in her bestselling book, Dead Aid, aid to Africa is not only not working – it has been positively harmful.

Vast inflows of Western aid money have distorted fragile local economies. They have pushed up the price of local goods and services, often pricing local would-be entrepreneurs out of their own local economy.

It is sometimes rather condescendingly implied that recipient countries are corrupt and that aid money is siphoned off by rent seekers trying to get their share of the aid pie. Of course it happens.

But it is less often pointed out that direct government-to-government assistance encourages corruption in the first place. It would be pretty extraordinary given the conditions Western aid policy creates if there was not corruption. We have managed to create precisely the conditions that allow the endemic corruption we say we abhor to flourish.

If you pay for more government, you tend to get more government. Western governments have spent a colossal $2 trillion encouraging the growth of government in Africa, rather than social and economic development.

Recipient governments like Uganda and Malawi have for most of the past decade received about a quarter of their annual income from the UK government. British officials in London are the single biggest source of income.

So to whom are the governments of Uganda or Malawi accountable? Does paying their government's bills make them inwardly accountable to people living in Uganda or Malawi? Or does it make them outwardly accountable to the international donor community?

Not long ago, Malawi's then President, Bingu wa Mutharika, bought himself a $16 million jet. Perhaps the poor fellow needed it to take him to meet with all those international aid donors that pay his government's bills. Maybe you prefer to see it as a rash purchase in a country where the average income is $810 a year.

But as long as Western governments pick up the tab, the one group of people who will never be allowed to answer that question are ordinary folk living in Malawi.

For six decades we have persisted in doing the wrong thing to help Africa. The 'experts' have failed to see that their lack-of-capital theory has it the wrong way round; a lack of savings, capital and domestic investment are as much a symptom of underdevelopment as its cause.

Africa is not underdeveloped merely because she lacks capital. As Gervais Williams puts it in *Slow Finance*, emerging nations do not become developed nations simply because they start to have access to capital.[68] Dogma stopped us from seeing this sooner.

Perhaps Western aid is not merely a matter of dogma. Maybe it is a form of indulgence, too. In medieval Europe, papal pardons were purchased for the remission of sin. In our own time, perhaps Western nations give aid to buy their way to virtue, too.

VESTED INTERESTS

'But if it was so obvious that a particular approach wasn't working, the experts would try another,' you say. 'They are not stupid.'

Indeed, most experts are far from stupid. The problem is, as Upton Sinclair observed, that 'it is difficult to get a man to understand something when his job depends on not understanding it'.

Too often those who ought to recognise that a particular approach or premise is flawed seem unable to do so because they have a vested interest in the system that keeps producing the wrong results.

If you are paid to promote the idea of publicly subsidised mortgages, you are unlikely to enhance your career prospects by pointing out that what you are doing is fruitless. Not only could federal officials at

HUD not see that Fannie Mae's lending policies were the cause of a massive housing bubble, officials used selective data to advocate ever more reckless lending targets. It suited them to muddle cause and effect.

No one working at the Environment Agency ever got fired for talking about 'flood risk ... rising sea levels ... climate change ... blah blah'. And for then preventing development. So officials stuck with ticking the boxes – and turning down the development because that is what the ticked boxes told them.

If you pick up a £150,000-a-year salary managing the local health service bureaucracy, you are not being paid to ponder why, with most British households within easy reach of a 24/7 supermarket, there are almost no family doctors open on a Saturday. So you stick with the dogma that insists government provides these things best.

As an 'aid expert', inflating the budget you administer next year is important. Informing the folk back home that the money you already spent has been wasted is not. So you big up how your aid programme is transforming Africa, and attack as heartless anyone suggesting anything different.

Government officials with an interest in government programmes are often left to judge the effectiveness of government programmes. And they turn out to be well positioned to argue in support of perpetuating what they do regardless of the strength of objective evidence. They are, after all, the 'experts', aren't they?

Why, having sunk such large sums into fruitless aid programmes, did no one suggest a different approach? How come no one suggested that, instead of throwing billions of dollars in aid, Western governments could simply forgo the same amount of revenue by not taxing trade with Africa?

Without tariff barriers, African producers could have sold directly to Western consumers. Africa is able to produce a bounty of food, agricultural goods, flowers, fish – precisely the sort of produce Western nations' protectionist trade policies seek to keep out. Imagine how Africa might be prospering today if, instead of $2 trillion grants, we allowed $2 trillion of tariff exemptions.

But of course forgoing $2 trillion revenue by not taxing trade with Africa does not require a grand design – or any well-remunerated designers. It would mean fewer aid experts and less officialdom. So aid experts and officials somehow never get around to suggesting it.

Instead of sluicing billions of dollars into high-risk debts in order to help disadvantaged Americans on to the property ladder, why did the housing experts not instead advocate giving low-income households tax breaks? Lift millions of Americans on to the housing ladder by lifting them out of taxation? Because tax breaks do not require federal programmes to administer. A federal programme does. So the administrators favour the latter, rarely ever the former.

As Francis Rouke put it, 'bureaucratic services generate constituents that oppose their liquidation'. Not only do public officials have a vested interest in reinforcing failure. External vested interests often urge them to stick with the status quo approach – even when things are clearly not working as they were supposed to.

Take the Western aid industry, again. Non-governmental aid agencies and charities – those

Graham Hancock once described as the 'Lords of Poverty' – often form a symbiotic relationship with government agencies. Drive around downtown Kampala or Nairobi, and the streets are full of 4x4s ferrying Western aid experts from one air-conditioned office to another. What interest do you suppose they have in explaining that using public money to develop Africa does not work?

Many such NGOs benefit either directly or indirectly from handouts of public money. Christian Aid has received €27 million of public money from EU officials as part of the West's international development budget over the past four years – although very little of that has actually been spent alleviating poverty in less developed countries. Such NGOs are hardly likely to be critical of an approach to aid that funds them.

Public officials and external vested interests often form alliances to extract money from the taxpayer – and lobby against change. It suits public officials to carry on spending Western aid budgets, however ineffectively. And it suits various corporate charity interests to work with those officials to make the case for bigger budgets.

How often are we told that 'all the experts agree'? If by 'all the experts', you mean all those public officials and corporate interests keen to see more public money spent in a particular field in a certain way, they seem to agree most of the time. But that does not make them right.

Experts, it is often implied, are disinterested specialists, with a detailed knowledge of a subject. More often they turn out to have a vested interest in what the rest of us think about a certain subject.

CHAPTER 6

THE ECONOMIC CONSEQUENCES OF ECONOMISTS

*The curious task of economics is to demonstrate to men
how little they really know about what they imagine they
can design.*
Friedrich Hayek

If only most economists shared Hayek's view. Alas,
many of those who profess to be economic experts
seem to believe they know much and can design a great
deal.

Yet it turns out that they are as vulnerable to false
premise and dogma as every other kind of expert who
believes in organising human affairs by grand design.

There is no shortage of economists today who believe
that an economy can be directed by deliberate design.

Since the financial crisis struck the West in 2008,
economists have been handed free rein to try to deal
with it, as they attempt to engineer growth on a gargan-
tuan scale. There has just not been much growth to
show for it.

In the United States, three massive fiscal stimulus
initiatives worth a grand total of some $1.4 trillion
have not only exhausted the US taxpayer – they have

exhausted almost every school of economic thinking that said you could engineer growth. From George Bush's $158 billion tax cut stimulus, to Barack Obama's $1,250 billion spending stimulus, every theorist has had their turn. And failed.

The biggest stimulus effort in history has failed to stimulate. Output growth remains modest. All those theories seem to have come to a very costly nothing. It is not only in America where the economists have failed.

In Britain, since 2007 there has been a more modest £390 billion mini fiscal stimulus. Europe, too, has seen various governments spend more than they raise in taxes in order to stimulate growth and create jobs, albeit perhaps not on quite the same scale. Successive Japanese administrations have tried deficit financing to stimulate the economy for almost a quarter of a century. Enormous amounts have been spent on boosting aggregate demand, and in 2009 Japan had yet another go, in the form of a ¥10 trillion spending spree.

All across the developed world, we have tested to destruction that idea that a fiscal stimulus is the way to engineer growth. It is not just fiscal engineering that has failed. Economists have tested to destruction the idea that monetary stimulus creates sustainable growth too – wrecking the West's monetary system in the process.

While those economists who favour fiscal stimulus have been allowed to let rip with every tool they could wish for, those that favour monetary stimulus have been given a free hand to manipulate monetary policy in pursuit of growth.

In the US, the Fed cut interest rates to almost zero – and has even promised to hold them there until at least 2013. In Japan and Britain, too, interest rates have been kept close to zero for years to try to bolster demand. At the same time, in Britain and America, government has printed billions of extra pounds and dollars (quantitative easing). To put it in context, for every $1 in circulation at the start of the crisis, there is now $2.30 in existence.[69]

Never before has economic policy been left so entirely to the experts, central bankers and the economists. Never before have we deferred so completely to those who claim that they can engineer growth. Every monetary lever has been tugged. Every billion-dollar button pressed.

But it has comprehensively failed. The West has started to slide back into recession.

What was it that made us believe that economists could engineer economic growth in the first place?

With very few exceptions, economists failed to see the financial meltdown coming. Many failed to recognise the crisis even as it was happening. What is remarkable is that we should have left it to such people to try to solve a crisis they not only failed to see coming, but have failed even now fully to explain.

It is perhaps not surprising that economists should believe that they can engineer the economy. There are, of course, many different schools of economic theory. Yet apart from a tiny number of free market economists, they all presume that growth can be engineered.

Some, like John Maynard Keynes, believe that during downturns, economic growth can be engineered by spending more. Others believe that it can be achieved by taxing less. Others emphasise not fiscal stimulus, but monetary – the idea that growth can be achieved by more credit. Different economists dispute the circumstances in which one might pull either the fiscal or the monetary levers and to what ends.

But what is so striking is the extent to which the 'official mind' in Europe, Britain, America and Japan almost universally accepts the idea that the level of demand in an economy *can and should be managed in the first place.*

Is this faith in demand management and growth by design justified?

Keynes's own ideas about using fiscal policy to manage demand implicitly suppose that experts are better at deciding what to do with people's private incomes than the individuals who earned it. Left to their own devices, suggested Keynes, people might save too much when they ought to be spending. Even if they do spend, imply some Keynesian economists, they cannot be trusted to spend it on the right sort of thing.

Keynes himself well understood that governments can only sustain present spending in excess of what they earn in tax out of past savings or future savings. Yet there are today many in the West who advocate a form of debauched Keynesianism. They not only think that government is better at spending money than individual people, but, they argue, government should carry on trying to stimulate demand by spending without ever trying to balance the books at all.

'When the facts change,' said John Maynard Keynes, 'I change my mind.' After throwing billions of dollars at failed fiscal stimulus, perhaps it is time for economists to change their minds about Keynesian economics – both the debauched version and the original.

Keynes maintained that raising demand within an economy would increase output and make it grow. But perhaps an economy does not grow because demand is increased. Maybe demand rises because an economy grows.

Aid experts mistakenly see a lack of capital in less developed countries as a cause of underdevelopment, when it is in fact a consequence. Similarly, many expert economists get the relationship between demand and economic growth the wrong way round, too.

There is already an almost insatiable appetite in almost every human society on earth for an infinite supply of consumer goods, gadgets, fashion items, improved housing and so on. That demand can only be actualised by real consumers willing to pay for all those extra goods and services because the productive output of the economy rises.

Might it be that the Keynesian presumption on which so much of the West's approach to economics is now based has it the wrong way round? Certainly the failure of the fiscal stimulus in America, Britain and Japan would suggest this might be the case.

Straightforward error. Big, complicated mistake.

If it is debauched Keynesians who have spent the past five years telling us that injecting extra money into the economy would make it grow, it is perhaps the debauched monetarist school of economics that has spent the past twenty years supposing that extra credit would make us prosper. The former economists have failed to get us out of the mess. The latter landed us in it.

Instead of merely using fiscal policy to direct the economy, debauched monetarism saw central bankers like Alan Greenspan using monetary policy to stimulate consumer demand, direct house prices and shore up equity bubbles.

Artificially low interest rates and cheap credit might have stimulated short-term growth. But they left banks hopelessly overextended, asset markets distorted and sovereign states bust.

Cheap credit encouraged us to consume and borrow beyond our means. Cheap credit created an addiction to yet more cheap credit. Or what Detlev Schlichter terms the 'forty-year credit boom'.

Eventually it had to come to an end. That overblown credit bubble had to burst. The pile of candy floss credit turned out to be mostly made of air. Sooner or later, the amount of credit will have to equal the underlying pool of savings. Consumption will have to reflect real incomes.

The deleveraging, default and debt deflation will be unavoidable – whatever the economists who landed us in this mess do to delay the consequences of their reckless designs.

Decades of leaving it to the expert economists and central bankers left us with boom built on bogus credit – and a massive, catastrophic crash.

Worse, every time the consequences of credit manipulation seemed about to come home to roost, the monetary manipulators have given the economy another shot of cheap credit.

Look back at the past two or three decades. In 1987, Black Monday saw stocks fall dramatically. Rates were cut to keep credit cheap. The Mexican crisis in 1994, rates cut. Long Term Capital Management collapsed 1998, ditto. Russia default, likewise. Asian flu 1999. You guessed it. Dot com bubble burst? 9/11? Ditto.

After years of keeping the price of credit artificially low, and encouraging a credit bubble to build up, eventually in August 2007 banks ran out of credit. But since the credit crunch hit, guess what the central bankers have done to try to fix things? Even lower rates.

Far from making things better, the lower rates that the economists and academics called for were responsible for one boom–bust cycle after another. Each time the Fed, at the urging of the experts, responded with yet another rate cut, it simply created a bigger bubble for next time round.

Every shot of cheap credit masked the decline in the Western world's underlying competitiveness. Every new fix caused what economists call 'malinvestment' – the artificially cheap money triggering unsustainable economic activity that for a while looked like real growth.

You cannot cure a patient by giving him more of what made him ill. Eventually you cannot cut interest rates any lower. You cannot prop up demand artificially and call it economic growth. Eventually all that bogus credit must eventually come out of the system. That day is now.

If economic growth could be engineered by fiscal and monetary manipulation, America, Britain, Japan and much of Europe would be riding high on a sea of prosperity. Instead, spending money we do not have has caused a massive and catastrophic accumulation of debt. Far from solving the credit crisis, having low interest rates has simply made the supply of real credit ever more scarce.

Instead of dealing with a debt crisis by saving more and spending less, the expert economists have encouraged the West to pile debt upon debt. Rather than cutting back overconsumption by consuming less, the experts have done everything they can to stoke up more consumption.

How much worse do things need to get before we abandon the idea that experts are able to engineer prosperity? Monetarist or Keynesian, debauched or pure, perhaps the real problem is having economists trying to direct the economy in the first place.

Why did we not see that the economists were getting so much so wrong for so long?

Because until things started to get really bad, we left it to the experts.

Leaving it to experts produced a micro housing disaster in Brooklands, Essex. If there was no mechanism able to swiftly put right one single misguided approach to planning rules in one tiny part of England, what chance would there be to put right a whole tranche of flawed assumptions about the entire Western political economy?

If it took a massive multi-billion-dollar market correction to show that the federal wise guys were simply wrong to presume that they could increase home ownership by giving cheap loans to people with no incomes, what might it take to show that the Fed has been making wrong-headed assumptions about the market economy?

Conventional economists are the last people to call time on conventional economics.

Economists, unsurprisingly, are attracted to the idea that economists know what is best, that they can engineer prosperity. The Keynesian presumption that economists can direct the economy by managing demand permeates Western government, central banks and universities precisely because it is so flattering to economists.

To be fair, there are a growing number of academics and others prepared to criticise conventional economics. But too often when they do so, they do so on the basis that conventional economists have failed to take into account what they regard as irrational human behaviour.

It is the people who are flawed, imply the fashionable new school of behavioural economists. It is the 'cognitive dissonance' of the masses that leaves them holding beliefs at odds with the evidence. Much less often do they conclude that it might not be the people who are flawed but the 'experts' and their grand theories, into which the rest of us so often refuse to fit.

Economists on the payroll of government also have a tendency to flatter government. Almost every proposal put forward since 2007 to stimulate Western economies through a fiscal stimulus has involved the government spending more, rather than taxing less. Just as aid 'experts' favour spending money on Africa, rather than forgoing taxes on trade with Africa, many economists somehow always seem to favour more spending to put money into the economy, rather than lower taxes in order not to take it out in the first place.

There is no shortage of vested interests – large banks and financial institutions – with a stake in demanding public handouts too. A bank in the business of making loans has a vested interest in cheap money to lend on to borrowers. In Britain, some of the most resolute defenders of the government's loose monetary policy have been banks that benefit from having lots of cheap credit to lend out. The prejudices of officialdom are reinforced by the vested interests of those in line for a bailout.

It is becomes very difficult to challenge vested interests once the dogma they, and the priesthood of economists, promote has become an article of faith. Often it is only the market that can correct things – and the market is about to do so on a massive scale.

GÖTTERDÄMMERUNG

Fiscal and monetary policies designed to stimulate economic growth in the West have not created growth. They have instead made a catastrophic mess of the West's fiscal and monetary affairs.

Fiscal policy has steadily shifted the burden of taxation in the West from taxes on consumption to taxes on the fruit of productive activity. Incomes are taxed, profits taxed, employment taxed.

Monetary policy has encouraged overconsumption, excessive debt, too little saving and not enough productive activity. With almost zero interest rates, thrifty Peter is punished and helping pay towards feckless Paul's excessive borrowing.

The economic consequences of doing what smart opinion in the universities, treasuries and central banks urged are proving to be catastrophic. Even now, the West is only just waking up to how much damage has been done as this man-made economic disaster begins to envelop us.

Holding rates low created chronic malinvestment – money being invested in things it never should have been invested in. Had the price of credit not been artificially lowered, many of the unsustainable investments that were started up would never have been allowed to get off the ground. The cost in economic and human misery of their inevitable failure and bankruptcies will be enormous.

Low rates caused a bubble in asset prices, bringing immense long-term harm. There is also good evidence that they helped lower productivity.

Perhaps low rates also distorted Western economies by encouraging labour to be replaced with capital. This forced down wages, helped export low-paid jobs abroad and – ironically – helped import low-paid workers into the West.

Perhaps those expert economists weren't so smart after all.

Decades of trying to stimulate growth by raising demand have left the West overconsuming, heavily in debt and reliant on imports. This did not just happen by accident. It was a consequence of letting economists try to direct the economy by deliberate design.

'For decades before the financial crisis in 2008, advanced economies were losing their ability to grow by making useful things' is how Raghuram G. Rajan puts it. 'In an effort to pump up growth, governments spent more than they could afford and promoted easy credit to get households to do the same. The growth that these countries engineered, with its dependence on borrowing, proved unsustainable.'[70]

Both the engineers and their engineering schemes have failed.

The unproductive West has priced itself out of the world markets – countries like Germany that have refrained from quite so much monetary and fiscal manipulation perhaps a little less so. In Britain and America, millions of low-paid jobs have been exported to low-cost countries, while millions of low-paid workers have been imported to work in high-cost Western countries.

Japan has had a quarter of a century of grand plans to stimulate the economy. And a quarter of a century of decline in her active labour force, rising debt, few new products and relative economic decline.

Western nations are losing their competitiveness, weighed down by debt and taxes. According to data compiled by the World Economic Forum, not only are the United States, Britain and France starting to fall down the rankings of global competitiveness, but emerging countries are catching up fast. Wealth creation is moving.

America has seen median incomes stagnating over the past two decades, with the average household earning in 1989 the same inflation-adjusted amount which they earn today. US standards of living have risen largely because Americans have borrowed, not earned, in order to consume more. And since the end of the dot com bubble, Americans have borrowed against rising property prices. It is not just subprime borrowers who turn out to be a lot less rich than they thought they were.

What were within living memory some of the greatest capitalist countries on earth – America and Britain – now depend on other people's capital to survive.

Nor should one overlook the role of economists and central bankers in the great banking crisis, either. It was economists and central bankers that helped draw up rules that encouraged banks to take risks. It was they who put in place rules that assumed sovereign debt was a safe bet. It was their Basel banking rules that made banks appear to make record profits and seem a picture of physical fitness moments before the whole house of cards came crashing down.

It would be unfair to blame economists for every banking failure, but they helped write the rules that allowed the banksters to draw up their Ponzi scheme. And it was the same economists who were the first to urge that the rest of us should have to bail it out when it started to fall apart.

'But isn't it a little bold to declare Western economic policy bankrupt, Carswell?' you might ask. 'You seem pretty certain that the experts have it wrong and you are right.'

It is not me that says the Western economic model is bust. It is the maths that screams it. Another crisis is inevitable – because of, not despite, the remedies that have been promoted by the world's leading economists.

All the expert economists producing all the theories and plans can no longer hide the fact that the West is no longer producing enough wealth to sustain the Western model. Only massive unsustainable levels of borrowing made it seem otherwise – for a while.

CHAPTER 7

LEVIATHAN GOES BUST

We have been spending the future for half a century.
Theodoros Pangalos, deputy Prime Minister of Greece,
May 2012

In October 2011, Klaus Regling, head of the European bailout fund, flew to China to ask for a loan. Regling's aim was to try to persuade Beijing officials to put as much as $700 billion of their $3.2 trillion foreign exchange reserve into the European bailout fund.

Just another sign of how power has shifted from West to East, you might think. More evidence of how interconnected our globalised world economy now is, eh.

But look at it another way.

Regling was asking a country with an annual income of $4,382 per head to lend money to a continent with an annual income of $32,615 per head. What kind of economic theory is it that ends up expecting China, where the average worker earns $80 a week, to bail out a society in which one in five of the working population is paid a good deal more than $80 a week to not work? You don't have to be an expert economist to see the flaw.

Something has got to give – and it won't be the Chinese, who after listening to Regling politely, sent him away empty-handed.

The West has not merely run out of money. Its big government political economy is bust.

THE SCALE OF THE WESTERN DEBT CRISIS

The global financial crisis is not really global. It is a Western crisis.

Nor is the West's financial crisis just about greedy banks. Nor, despite being first manifest as a subprime crisis, was it caused by folk living in Alabama shacks taking out loans they could not repay.

The West is in a financial mess because governments have been living beyond the productive capacity of their economies to sustain them for years. Like someone running up a credit card bill because they spend more than they earn, the US government has run up a debt of $15 trillion, the Japanese $13.6 trillion, the UK $2 trillion and the Eurozone countries $11.8 trillion.

This is what that total debt (black) looks like when compared to annual income (grey).

Public debt and GDP

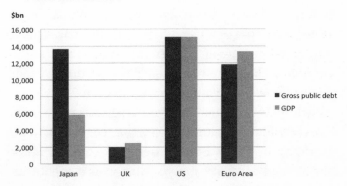

'Don't worry,' say the experts. 'This is all about imbalances in the world economy. China and Co. might be making everything and the West importing it all on borrowed money. But it will sort itself out,' they cheerfully tell us.

'These imbalances', runs the theory, 'are all due to the Chinese saving too much.' Because they lack a 'social security net', the Chinese prefer to hoard what they earn, rather than blow it on flat-screen TVs like they should.

But sooner or later, the experts insist, the Chinese will emulate us and have the kind of big, bloated social security 'safety net' that will free them to spend, spend, spend. Once their government becomes as big and bloated as our own, the global economy will be back in equilibrium.

But what if it is the other way round? What if it is not their governments that have to get bigger, but ours that must get dramatically smaller? Does it not occur to the experts that it is not China that will have begun to emulate Western consumption habits, but the West that will have to scale back its bloated government?

If you are waiting for China to create a system of welfare that pays one in five householders to sit at home and watch daytime TV, you could be waiting a long time. The money for bloated Western welfarism will run out long before Shanghai adopts the Swedish model of universal benefits or Obama Care.

Back in 1960-something, you could afford to have a government consume 30–40 per cent GDP. The competition – Italy, Britain, Germany – weren't that far behind. But what happens when your competitors have governments that only take up 25 per cent of their GDP (Mexico), or a 20 per cent state (India), or even a 17 per cent state (Brazil)? How do you create the wealth to pay for your 40 per cent Western welfare state then?

France currently spends 30 per cent of her national wealth on welfare entitlements. Germany spends 27 per cent and Britain 22 per cent. South Korea spends less than 10 per cent. China, India and Indonesia even less.[71] In which countries has output expanded faster in recent years? Even if China's overdue credit contraction leads to a sharp contraction in output, as I fear it will, what do you think of as a better long-term bet for growth?

There are indeed trade imbalances. But these imbalances are a symptom of the problem, not the actual problem. Western nations have been importing cheap Chinese goods on credit because Western states have been stimulating massive, unsustainable overconsumption using various fiscal and monetary tools.

'The fault, dear Brutus, lies not in our stars.' Nor even in China. But in ourselves.

Official statistics on debt-to-GDP ratios make unpleasant reading. But they do not tell the full, grim story.

As a constituency MP, over the years folk have come to see me at my regular advice surgeries with debt problems. They usually come to see me when they can't cope. Husbands have run up credit card debts. Wives remortgaged the house to pay for a lifestyle their family income could not sustain.

As I sit listening to each tragic tale, there's one part

of the story that always runs the same: they somehow always managed to fool themselves that the debt wasn't as big as it actually was, and that their ability to pay it back was greater than it turned out to be.

Western countries are doing exactly the same. Firstly, we have been understating the real size of our debts.

Take Britain as an example. Our official debt stands at £900 billion, or 60 per cent of national income. Except it isn't. The real level of debt is not only that 'official debt'. By any normal standards of accounting it ought to also include unfunded future liabilities. Looked at that way, the UK's level of debt is even greater.

Add in all those things we are going to have to pay for, but have not saved for, and UK debt is £3.6 trillion, or 244 per cent of national income.[72] How come there's such a gap between the official statistics and the real level of debt?

The official data does not include pesky things like all those future unfunded public pension obligations, estimated to amount to something like £1.1 trillion – or 78 per cent of GDP. It is rather like having a second national debt alongside the official one. It already costs us £32 billion a year, more than we spend on policing, law and order, courts and prisons combined.[73] In a few years, it is likely to cost more than we spend on defence.[74]

Then there are all those 'off-balance sheet' things we've been spending (a further £1.35 trillion) and the cost of bailing out all those zombie banks (another £1.34 trillion). Tot it all up, and Britain is looking pretty broke.

THE TRUE SCALE OF BRITAIN'S DEBT

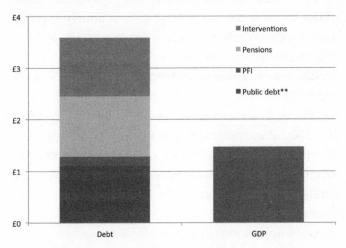

Source: Tullett Prebon, *Thinking the Unthinkable*

Germany's debt-to-GDP ratio seems like a sensible 60-something per cent. Perfectly manageable, you might think. Until you add in the unfunded pension liabilities and realise that it is then over 250 per cent of GDP.

In America, too, the real level of debt is much higher than the $15 trillion official figure once you start to add in future unfunded liabilities.

Although it might sound implausible, given that US public debt is officially $15 trillion, some analysts, such as Lawrence Kotlikoff, have estimated that the US government has unfunded liabilities of one kind or another of over $100 trillion, or almost a quarter of a million dollars for every American.[75]

Just as debtors tend to understate their debts, they also have a habit of overstating their ability to pay them back by overstating their future income. Western governments are no different.

The higher a country's GDP – or annual income – the easier it ought to be to pay off any debts. But the trouble is that GDP figures show us a very distorted view of a country's real ability to generate wealth to pay back what it owes.

If a farmer grows a hundred apples, and sells them for £100, Britain's GDP increases by £100. The total wealth of the country will have increased by £100. But if the government spends £100, the GDP statistics records that expenditure as a £100 increase in GDP. But has that government spending really increased the total wealth of the country by £100? GDP data makes no distinction between government spending money it does not have, and real wealth creation.

A lot of the data on GDP – especially in Western states with big public sectors – is a measure of the government's propensity to spend, not the economy's ability to produce wealth. Indeed, it is often a measure of the government's propensity to spend money it does not actually have.

Just like the debtor who comes to see me in my constituency surgeries, Western states are pretending that they owe less than they really do, and banking on the ability to earn future incomes that they might not be able to earn.

Imagine if, like one of my indebted constituents, you earned, say, £30,000 a year. But you owe 120 per cent of that – £36,000. Not an impossible situation to manage, you might think. Pay back a little bit each year, and after 15, 20, 25 years, you should be clear.

But what if the debt of £36,000 turns out to be growing each year because you still spend more than you earn? Governments in America, Britain, Japan and most of Europe continue to live beyond what they earn in tax each year.

Worse, what if you also find that the interest payments on the debt you need to make are growing the debt faster than you are paying it back? What if, like those faltering Western economies, you find that the debt is expanding faster than your economy is growing?

Or, what if you find that your annual income of £30,000 is actually a lot closer to £25,000, because – like Western GDP data – you had been overstating your earning capacity?

Many Western states seem hooked on debt. This is not because Western governments have temporarily adopted deficit spending to help them cope with hard times. *Years of deficit spending have produced the hard times.*

Between 2009 and 2011, the 111th US Congress ran up more debt in two years than the first hundred US Congresses combined managed to between 1789 and 1989. In 2010, the American government was borrowing $100 billion each month.

In the United States, the federal government spent $600 billion in 1965. In 2008, federal spending had risen to $3 trillion (at constant 2007 prices).

In the early 1980s, the United States was the world's largest creditor nation, and Americans saved on average a tenth of their incomes.[76] Today, the average American family has a mere $7,500 savings, but $661,410 of public and private debts.[77]

When Europe's Klaus Regling went to China to borrow money to fund that gap between what Europe spends and what she earns, he was simply doing what America has done for the past thirty years. America's government is borrowing the equivalent of the total output of Canada every year, just to pay the bills – mostly by writing out IOUs to China. A country where millions of folk are barely out of rice paddies is lending money to keep Americans supplied with iPads – and making them too.

Rather like constituents of mine who find themselves caught in a spiral of debt, America is going to have to pay impossibly large sums in order to keep her creditors satisfied. By 2020, America will need to spend between 15 and 20 per cent of tax revenues simply servicing all that debt – more than she spends on defence. 'The superpower will have evolved from a nation of aircraft carriers', in Mark Steyn's phrase, 'to a nation of debt carriers'.[78]

By 2030, 36 per cent of tax revenues will be needed to pay the interest. By 2040, 58 per cent, and by 2050, 85 per cent. By 2055, interest payments on the debt might actually exceed total federal revenue. Of course it will never get to that. Something will give long before it reaches that stage.

By 1788, Louis XVI's government in Paris was spending 60 per cent of its tax revenue on debt servicing. It is not a comforting precedent.

It is not just America. Britain's political economy, too, is hooked on debt. Since 2003, Britain's public administration has had a long-term dependence on borrowing something like 10 per cent of GDP each year.[79] In the years before the recession, Britain's political economy ran a system that borrowed £2.18 for every £1 of growth.[80]

For all the talk of austerity in Britain, the coalition government is not struggling to pay off its debts. It is not even close to being able to start paying anything back. It is still struggling, without much success, to slow down the rate at which Britain's borrowings keep on increasing, while adding more than £100 billion more to public debt each year.

Across the Eurozone, government spending is more than 50 per cent of GDP, while government revenues are about 44 per cent of GDP.[81]

Western states seem unable to help themselves. Look at how almost every Western government has raised taxes since 2008 to – we are told – tackle the deficit. Taxes certainly went up, but what happened to the extra money that was scooped in? Was it used to pay down the debt, like the tax raisers solemnly promised? Not at all. Any extra tax was spent. In almost every Western country higher taxes have been accompanied by even more borrowing and spending. It is as if Big Government just can't stop itself.

The only Western states that are not broke seem to be those that somehow kept government small (South Korea or Australia) or managed to shrink it (Finland, Estonia or Sweden).

THE END OF THE ROAD

Western governments grew big by hiding the costs of more government.

Unequal taxes allowed the burden of all that official-dom to be shared unequally. Monetary manipulation allowed wealth to be transferred from the private to the public sector via inflation tax. And governments borrowed enormous amounts via the bond markets and 'off balance sheet' too.

But the financial crisis marks the end of the road for this twentieth-century way of running Western society.

In 2010, America was selling $100 billion of Treasury IOUs each month to pay her way.

But for how much longer?

It is inevitable that the United States government will have to live within the United States tax base sooner or later.

In 2006, the seventeen members of the Eurozone borrowed €5.8 trillion. Just four years later, they borrowed €7.8 trillion – an increase approaching 40 per cent.[82] With so much euro debt circulating, many potential lenders already have more than they want. Many have stopped lending – or started to demand extortionate rates for doing so.

Already the arithmetic of the bond market has begun to strip some Western states of their ability to live beyond their tax base by borrowing. Greece can no longer borrow any money on the open market. Italy, Portugal, Spain and Belgium might not be able to for much longer.

'But bonds are cheap,' you say. 'America, Britain and Germany have never been able to borrow more money more cheaply. In fact, investors are pretty much paying to invest in UK government debt.'

True. The fact that some Western nations are no longer able to borrow money has helped push down the cost of borrowing for other heavily indebted Western nations that are seen as more reliable debtors.

But another way of looking at this bond bubble phenomenon is that almost all Western states have to be lent cash to fund their massive overspending habits. Some are still able to carry on writing out the IOUs, others are not.

Eventually the cost of borrowing all that money

from China, cash-rich Asia and sovereign wealth funds will rise. The bond bubble will eventually burst.

Greece might be the first Western country to discover that you cannot keep running up debts to pay for a lifestyle you do not earn. She will not be the last. The laws of mathematics are universal.

Underlying many of the assumptions about Western debt levels is the belief that governments – at least Western ones – do not go bust. However many zillions of dollars, pounds or yen they might owe, runs the conventional thinking, they can always simply print off more and inflate away their debts.

That has been true in the past. But can we be so certain it will be in the future?

Any Western state that started to do that now would find it much harder to borrow. America, Britain and other Western states are only able to borrow from international lenders because the lenders have confidence that they will be paid back in a currency that is not ravaged by inflation. If Western states start to use inflation to erode the value of existing debt, who would be prepared to extend further debts to them?

And if a government was to simply print more money, what might it mean for the future of that currency?

Until 1971, Western governments could not simply print as much money as they liked. Under the Bretton Woods agreement, the number of US dollars in circulation was linked to the amount of gold the US Treasury had. And the value of the pound – and most other Western currencies – was linked to the US dollar.

But forty years ago, the US broke the link to gold. Since then, the number of dollars, or pounds, or yen in circulation has been entirely a matter decided by the respective governments of America, Britain and Japan. Western currencies have become fiat, or paper only, currencies.

Start to print too much paper money, and pretty quickly it begins to have the value of mere paper.

Governments in America, Britain, France and even Japan, as well as Italy, Greece and Portugal, find themselves addicted to spending more than they earn. For years they have borrowed to make up the difference.

They will not be able to borrow in the next decade or so as they have in the decades past. Unable to keep borrowing, or even inflating their way out of debt, government is soon going to have to get smaller.

'Not going to happen,' you retort. 'There are no mainstream politicians proposing to shut down large swathes of government. Besides, no one is going to vote for this.'

Perhaps not. But it is the laws of mathematics, not the laws made by politicians, that will count. No one in Greece voted to slash public spending or shut down large swathes of the Greek government. But that is what happened. The laws of maths eventually prevail.

Government throughout the Western world is going to have to dramatically shrink. Political will might decide how and by what means government is scaled down. Politics might determine if it is a soft landing, without casualties, or a crash. But down the size of government is going to have to go.

Ultimately, perhaps the politicians and the technocratic elite who landed us in this mess will be so discredited that it might not really matter what they propose to do about it.

THE CRISIS OF THE ELITES

We have not overthrown the divine right of kings to fall down for the divine right of experts.
Harold Macmillan

Go back five hundred years, and the source of authority in most Western states came from God – or his delegate, the King. When the world was deemed as divinely ordained, those ordained by the Divine ruled.

Reach back three hundred years, and God-given authority had weakened. Authority came no longer from God, but by virtue of class or inheritance. Those who ruled over society did so because they were considered to come from the ranks of those most capable of doing so.

Two hundred years ago, authority no longer came from the First Estate (the clergy) nor the Second (the nobility). It came increasingly from the Third Estate – the people. In fits and starts, aristocracy gave way to democracy; the idea of being governed by those of rank yielded to the notion that competition for votes would produce leaders of merit. Democracy came to be seen as a better way of producing an elite best able to govern.

But with our debauched democracy today, where is that wise, disinterested elite? Having overthrown the government of the clergy, we seem to be governed by a priesthood of technocrats instead.

The elite have devised ever grander schemes, organising ever more, from universal health care to education, to the economy and society itself. From early twentieth-century US Progressives, to mid-twentieth-century socialists, to Euro integrationists today, this elite have put their faith in the wisdom of people like themselves. They have venerated the power of the expert to order human affairs, despising as they do so the wisdom and the spontaneity of the market.

Yet trying to arrange Western societies by grand design has brought only ruin and failure. This priesthood has lurched from one crisis to another.

Central bankers' stewardship of the money has left us with a Ponzi pile of paper currency. Economists have stalled the economy. 'After decades of ongoing and generous expansion of the fiat money supply,' says Detlev Schlichter, 'of artificially low interest rates and cheap credit, banks are hopelessly overextended, asset markets are distorted, and sovereign states are bust.'

Just as medieval monks lived off the tithe, in our own age corporate bankers grew rich on the back of state handouts of credit. All across Europe and America, billions have been billed to the taxpayer to save bankers from the consequences of their own foolish investment decisions – and to save the technocrats' grand ambition of monetary union from reality.

As Charles Moore has put it, all across Europe we see the emergence of a 'money-power nexus' with unelected bankers at the helm.[83] In first Greece and then Italy, democratically elected governments were removed and replaced by unelected technocrats. Across Europe, democracy is being subverted by an alliance of big government and big businesses. An oligarchy.

And what did those that we vote for do about it? Nothing. At times in Britain perhaps they were too busy enriching themselves at public expense with tax-free 'second incomes' to care. Certainly too few of those that we elect to scrutinise the rich and the

powerful – and those who become rich by being powerful – seemed up to the job.

The authority of the First and the Second Estate
has crumbled. In our own age, the power of the Third
Estate – the people – has been subverted by debauched
democracy. But what about the power of the Fourth
Estate – the press? Surely those fearless campaigning
journalists were on the case?

It turns out that many pet media pundits were lazily
recycling established opinion rather than asking the
sort of questions that needed to be put. In Britain,
the phone-hacking scandal exposed the cosy collusion
between media moguls and the political elite. Far from
asking challenging questions, multinational media
barons, it seems, bought and bullied their way to establish control over party leaders, police, prosecutors and
regulators.

Central bankers, regulators, journalists, politicians
... the elite, together with their Hayekian intellectuals, have been inept. It is no longer possible to pretend
that the system of democracy we have today produces
a class of wise and capable experts presiding over the
rest of us.

This collapse in confidence in the elite can be measured empirically. While almost 90 per cent of Britons
trust doctors and over 80 per cent trust teachers, bankers are trusted by a mere 29 per cent, ministers by 17
per cent and politicians by 13 per cent.[84]

'It was ever thus,' you might say.

No it was not.

In 2000, most Britons believed that you could 'trust
a politician to tell the truth in a tight corner'. Today
only one in three would agree.[85] In 1987, over 90 per

cent said you could 'trust the government to put the national need first'. Today almost half disagree.[86]

In 1987, 91 per cent of people said they thought banks were well run. By 2009, only 19 per cent agreed.[87] In 1987, almost half of people trusted government, today it is a mere 16 per cent.[88]

There has been a haemorrhage of confidence in the elite – in politicians, central bankers, public officials and technocrats. An inept, self-serving, asinine oligarchy.

Not only is this is a crisis of the elite. It is a crisis for a political system that allowed them to govern us so disastrously. A meltdown for the body politic.

Contempt for elites only reaches this level on the eve of revolutions. Here it comes.

PART 2

THE BIRTH OF iDEMOCRACY

CHAPTER 8

THE DIGITAL REVOLUTION

First came the agricultural revolution. About 10,000 years ago, different groups of people living on different continents made the same discovery: they could grow crops and domesticate animals. It was transformative because it allowed *Homo sapiens* to feed himself without having to gather and hunt from the wild.

Then about 300 years ago came the industrial revolution. Starting in the Netherlands and England, it allowed both countries – and eventually most of the world – to escape those Malthusian constraints of famine and starvation. Able to harness the power of fossil fuel to increase the supply of food and productive capacity, the per capita wealth of humankind has risen almost every year since.

Now comes the third great technological revolution – the digital revolution. It started in the 1980s, with the mass application of digital logic circuits that allowed the storage, manipulation and sharing of vast quantities of information. We are only beginning to see the transformative impact that this will have on the way human societies are ordered and organised. Yet already we can see that it is going to turn many assumptions on their head.

The earlier revolutions saw humans learn how to harness first domesticated animals and plants, then fossil fuel. The digital revolution will transform our lives because it will allow us to harness collective human intelligence on a scale that has never been possible before.

A REAL REVOLUTION?

The word 'revolution' – which comes from the Latin *revolutio*, or the rotation of a wheel – is much over-used. But digital technology really will overturn many of the existing assumptions about how society is best organised.

COLLECTIVE INTELLIGENCE

Human beings, suggests Matt Ridley, the author of *The Rational Optimist*, can do something no other species manages: we can specialise, trade and exchange. 'Somewhere in Africa more than 100,000 years ago,' he writes, humankind 'began to add to its habits, generation by generation' thanks to the power of 'exchange … the swapping of things and services between individuals'.[89]

This has given humankind, he continues, 'an external, collective intelligence' far greater than anything we each might be able to hold in our own brain – however individually clever we might be.

You don't need to look very far to see that Ridley has a point.

Think of some of the everyday items in your home – a frozen pizza in the freezer or the smartphone sitting on your desk. If pushed to explain how such everyday items were made, I might be able to mutter something about wheat and olives (pizza) or silicon chips and plastic (smartphones).

But try to get me to make either a pizza or a smartphone from scratch, including mining or growing the raw ingredients, and I would find it impossible to explain the process in detail, let alone do it. In fact, no single human being could possibly make from scratch even a fraction of the everyday items in your home.

Yet there they are. Thanks to the ability of humans to specialise, trade and exchange, we can have an enormous array of things made for us, perhaps none of which were ever the product purely of one person working on their own, but of many hundreds, or even thousands.

This collective intelligence does a lot more than keep us stocked up on pizza and smartphones. It is what has produced everything from modern medicine and science to motor cars and houses. It is what makes humans unique – and it has been the driver of human progress down the ages.

The mass application of digital logic circuits exponentially increases the scope for human trade, exchange and specialisation. It not only enables much greater commercial exchange (think eBay or Amazon), but the free flow of ideas and wider kinds of collaboration on a previously unimaginable scale.

Collective intelligence is, if you stop to think about it, not just a pretty good description of Wikipedia. It is what you find each time you type in a Google search.

The digital age means an ever expanding possibility

by humans to share and exchange, to trade goods, services and ideas, and for an ever greater specialisation of labour.

... BUT WITHOUT DIRECTION FROM ABOVE

For much of human history, doing things collectively tended to boil down to having a small number of humans telling the rest what to do. Collective endeavour was not based on spontaneous exchange and transaction the way we in the West now take for granted, but on top-down determinism at best, coercion at worst.

Whether it was a pharaoh commanding slaves to build a pyramid or priests getting serfs to construct a cathedral, a tiny elite directed collective action from above.

Not surprisingly this tiny elite often, as Ridley puts it, 'predate upon and parasitize their fellows' productivity – to take and not to give'. Human progress was 'sporadically slowed, set back and reversed by the enervating greed of the parasites'.

Indeed, from Ming China to medieval Europe to the Maya, history is littered with societies where the parasitical elite came close to killing the system off which they fed.

The digital revolution will vastly expand the scope for humans to do what comes naturally to our species – to trade, exchange, collaborate and specialise. Greater collective endeavour will be possible, but with far less need to do it with direction from above. For perhaps the first time in 100,000 years, we will be able to do without the parasites because we will be able to organise ourselves collectively without the top-down designs that enable parasitism.

Think of the digital revolution as an insurgency against that long parasitical line – of priests and princes, and today of bureaucrats and politicians – that has leeched off human progress.

THE DIGITAL WORLD

'All this talk of a digital revolution is overblown,' a fellow MP barked at me recently in the House of Commons tea room. 'You might waste a lot of time on that Twitter-book thing, Carswell, but they are hardly going to change the world.'

Perhaps, you think, he has a point. It could be that by the time you read this, Twitter and Facebook have turned out to have been no more than a passing fad, like Bebo or MySpace before them. Perhaps.

There is, when it comes to technology, a tendency towards what the techies call 'macro myopia'. That is to say, to overestimate the impact of technology in the short run, but to underestimate the impact in the long run.

I suspect that many of the claims about how digital technology has changed everything have been overdone. Computers have not, despite all kind of claims and expectations, increased productivity significantly.[90] All that hype about a 'new business paradigm', which fuelled the dot com bubble, turned out to be just hype. There have been all sorts of absurdly overblown claims about how Twitter caused popular uprisings during the Arab Spring.

Rather than racing ahead, let us instead step back and examine a number of trends that we can already discern, and see how they might shape things.

The digital world means:

- **Things become more personalised – or 'hyper-personalised':** it is already clear that digital technology enables many more individuals to make many more personalised choices. From the music we listen to, to the TV we watch, digital means more self-selection. The digital market is more niche, better able to meet distinctive needs, and less generic.

- **Less reliance on experts:** with much more self-selection, we are beginning to rely less on other people making generic choices for us. This applies not just to music and entertainment. We already depend much less on having others select news, views and opinions for us, too. Self-selection means we will defer less to those experts who used to make these kinds of choices for us.

- **Less tendency to do things by grand designs:** when experts decide things, as we saw in Chapter 3, they have a tendency to try to do things by design. Giving experts a big role in human economic and social affairs therefore inclines us towards trying to arrange human affairs by design. But with less of a role for the expert, there will be far less of a tendency to do things by design.

  At the same time, given the organic nature of the internet, collectivism without the state will become possible in ways that were not previously practical.

- **Small becomes big:** the internet is starting to challenge a number of assumptions about size and scale in business and economics. Economy of scale, so long regarded as an objective in itself in business and economics, is not quite so important in a world of niche markets. For example, instead of looking to sell one music track to millions, the music business is able to profitably cater to many more niche tastes than before.

- **Small state advantage:** big is no longer necessarily beautiful in business – nor so when it comes to organising other aspects of human affairs. Big states no longer have the automatic advantage of having larger domestic markets and economies of scale that they used to, compared with smaller states.

- **The iTax base:** in a world where so much is just a mouse-click away, capital and know-how are hyper-mobile. This is going to test a number of assumptions about how much tax governments can collect, and how they can collect it.

- **Money in the internet age:** the internet means we can shop around for much more. It is starting to mean that we can shop around with, and use, all kinds of currencies. This will have an influence on how governments manage money – and their ability to manage money in their interest as a debtor.

Let us examine each of these trends in greater detail.

HYPER-PERSONALISED

Sneering at what he called 'that internet whatsit', my House of Commons colleague delivered his knock-out argument: 'My secretary', he declared, 'tells me that Twitter and Facebook are full of the most utterly banal and irrelevant chit-chat.'

I have often heard it pointed out that 99 per cent of other people's tweets and Facebook updates are trite, if not tedious. And to you and me and backbench MPs, they undoubtedly are. But that observation precisely misses the point.

Of course you will find most other people's Twitter traffic tedious. That is because it is their Twitter traffic, set up by them to follow those they – not you – find interesting. Twitter accounts are a personalised ticker-tape news feed set up for individuals.

Most people would find tweets about Beth's trip to the shops, or Sam's views about the Obama budget, or updates on Coldplay's tour dates a turn off. Which is why most people on Twitter do not follow Beth or Sam or @coldplay.

Twitter might seem glib and superficial, but it actually does something rather remarkable that will change the way we interact with the world and other people in it.

Cast your mind back to the time before Twitter or Facebook. You really don't need to go back that that far. Twitter launched in 2006, Facebook in 2004.

Before then how did you get to hear about things happening in the world beyond your front door?

Word of mouth, perhaps. Notice boards at school, work or college. Perhaps if you were keen to catch up on the latest gossip, you might hope to bump into friends of yours who were 'in the know'.

News about what was happening in the wider world perhaps came to you via a few dozen TV and radio channels, plus a dozen local or national newspapers.

You could, if you were a news junkie, watch, read and listen to them all. But for the most part, most people were fed a small sample of all the news stories that were out there. They were filtered for us by no more than a few hundred editorial staff, selecting what they thought of as newsworthy.

But then along came Facebook and Twitter.

They have transformed the way that news travels

and the way that we access information about what is happening in the world around us.

Facebook not only allows you to pass on information that you would once have had to read the work or college notice board for. It allows you to catch up on the kind of chat and gossip that you would once have picked up there, too.

Instead of editorial staff putting together a package of news stories, Twitter allows everyone to do the job themselves. We each create our own personalised news feed. Just like those ticker tape news feeds on City trading floors, your Twitter account becomes a sort of news ticker tape just for you. Instead of bringing you information about the price of shares, your Twitter account feeds you with updates about the sort of 'price movements' that interest you, from the ultra-micro (Beth's shopping trip) to the macro (what Barack Obama has to say about the global economy) to the in-between stuff (Coldplay's tour dates).

Imagine a TV news broadcast that led with those three items. Few would find them newsworthy. Most would switch off. Yet Twitter allows the few dozen people on the planet for whom those three bits of information are the most interesting bits of news to be broadcast direct to them.

The digital world is all of a sudden one in which everyone can pick their own settings – and not just when it comes to deciding which of your gossipy friends to follow on Twitter. On Twitter, we get the news we deserve. We can select what programmes our children watch on our own self-programmed TV (iPad). We can each have our own self-programmed radio station (Spotify or Napster). And just as you find other people's tweets of little interest, their Spotify playlist might not be much to your liking either.

Technology will influence popular culture and presumptions in ways we are only just beginning to understand.

I grew up in a world in which BBC producers selected most of the music that awkward adolescents listened to. Today, the digital revolution makes it possible to select not only all of the music we listen to for ourselves, but many of those things that we have always been used to have selected for us by experts. Increasingly, those in society and the economy who select things for us will find themselves redundant.

But it is not only those who select music and entertainment for us who will see their influence diminished. Those who select ideas and opinions for us are being displaced, too.

EXPERTS OVERTHROWN

On March 24 2009, Daniel Hannan stood up in the European Parliament in Brussels and spoke for three minutes. His speech attacking the then British Prime Minister, Gordon Brown, was one of dozens of speeches made in the chamber that afternoon. It was ignored by mainstream political pundits and not carried on any news channels. Hannan's opinions were not, in the view of the experts that select the news for us, worth passing on.

Then something strange happened.

A three-minute video of his speech was posted on to YouTube, and links to it started to be emailed around spontaneously. Within a few hours, it had been viewed by 40,000 people. Within a few days, it had been watched by over a million. Today it has been seen by almost 3 million people online.

In fact, it created such a sensation that the newsroom editors who had ignored it started to report the speech, in turn generating yet more interest.

What was as fascinating as the reaction of the public was the reaction of the British media elite.

Echoing the tone of many, Peter Wilby, former editor of the *New Statesman*, claimed that the fact that the Hannan speech went viral was proof that 'the internet lacks quality control'.

Wilby was, in a sense, right. Until the internet came along, we got our news via someone like Peter Wilby, or a BBC reporter. And so the news that we got was filtered through the prism of people like them, with all their prejudices and preconceptions.

It is not that the internet means there are no filters. We do not, generally, tend to spend hours browsing the web on the off chance that we will find a YouTube video of someone demolishing Gordon Brown. Most of those 2.9 million viewers on YouTube will have had the video recommended to them by someone else. The filters are built out of the collective intelligence of the crowd, not the wisdom of a tiny media elite. It is the everybody, rather than the likes of Peter Wilby, who get to decide what constitutes news – and for that matter, quality.

When Wilby complained about the quality of the speech, he was not protesting about Hannan's use of grammar. Rather, as Hannan has himself put it, for Wilby and Co. it was the 'content that was disagreeable. The quality filters he evidently had in mind would screen out points of view that he considers unacceptable: that taxes are too high, that present borrowing levels are unsustainable, that Britain would flourish outside the EU.'

Thanks to the internet it is no longer left to a tiny self-regarding elite to interpret things on our behalf, and feed us their opinions. As long as there are some more articulate than others, there will always be a class of commentators, but it has been democratised.

Bloggers have rudely interrupted the monopoly of the old elite commentariat. While old-school news-paper pundits have to face inwards to their editors at the morning conference meeting, bloggers face outward in pursuit of online clicks in a way no indi-vidual contributor, however much their newspaper is bought by paying customers, individually needed to do.

Pundits could – and very often did – make a career out of being wrong. So long as they were as wrong as every other pundit in the pack, they would soon build up a reputation for being a sensible sort. Today online readers simply stop reading their clichés. Many profes-sional pundits in Westminster have, I notice, quietly shifted their opinions about, say, immigration, Europe or government spending. And they have had to do so, precisely because they are losing the power to decide what views and ideas are or are not acceptable.

Perhaps it is because I am a politician that I first noticed the way that the internet is democratising comment and opinion forming in Westminster. But the more I look elsewhere, the more I see the same phenomenon at work, overturning established opinion and the priesthood of pundits who peddle it. No longer can those used to telling us how to see the world do so unchallenged.

For years, a small group of climate change experts

looked at the data that they had gathered – and then handed us their verdict. 'That set of temperature readings shows we're heading for rapidly rising temperatures,' they pronounced. 'And that data means it's even worse than we thought.'

Just like British politics, we left it to a small clique of experts to do the comment and analysis, whose wisdom seemed set in tablets of stone.

Until one day someone leaked all the emails from the Climate Research Centre at my alma mater, East Anglia University. Suddenly everybody could trawl through the data – and several hundred did. And some of them came to very different conclusions about what the facts actually meant.

Worse, others appeared to detect attempts by the 'experts' who had analysed the data to present it in a way that they felt was deliberately misleading.

Whatever you think about the climate change debate, and whatever the truth about the UEA data, it is difficult to deny that the disclosure of information online in that way had a profound impact on the whole subject. It galvanised sceptics to fight against any comprehensive deal at Copenhagen, and it put many established climate change advisers on the back foot. Some even suggest that the International Panel on Climate Change has yet to recover its credibility.

But this is not just about the UEA climate change controversy, or the changing status of pundits in Westminster. Each of these is a straw in the wind, evidence of a far bigger change that is coming; the internet has disintermediated comment and opinion. That is a fancy way of saying that it has taken out the middle man and his often fanciful ideas.

THE ENGINE OF STATISM STALLS

'The blogs and Twitter', said my pompous colleague in the House of Commons, 'are self-referential. Just lots of people talking about themselves and what interests them. An echo chamber.'

And what, I wondered, are MPs and all the other elite experts, if not self-referential? What are those who like to interpret the world for us, if not full of their own prejudices and presumptions?

It was Hayek who famously described how a tiny number of academics, broadcasters and officials recycled ideas and opinions, which soon became conventional wisdom. And it was Hayek, too, who saw how such people tended to favour doing things according to grand plans and designs.

Being intelligent and rational, thought Hayek, these experts overrated the ability of social and human affairs to be arranged by rational design. They were, in Hayek's clumsy phrase, constructive rationalists.

As we saw in Chapter 3, it was this – a tendency to do things by grand design – that accounts for the way in which the boundaries of public policy have grown ever greater. Concerns that were once regarded as matters for individuals, families or local communities have over the past century come to be seen as matters for experts and government to arrange by design.

In Chapters 4 and 5, we saw the extent to which this elite is able to make decisions regardless of what voters actually vote for. We saw the way they often make decisions on the basis of recycled dogma and ideas – and often carry on making wrong-headed decisions because they are driven by secondhand ideas.

The digital revolution is a coup d'état against the

tyranny of this elite. It overthrows these secondhand dealers in other people's ideas.

As Hayek saw, elite intellectuals owed much of their position to the fact that they came to hear of new ideas and theories ahead of the masses. They lose that advantage once everyone can read it on Twitter or the blogosphere too.

'Even though their knowledge may be often super-ficial', Hayek went on, 'and their intelligence limited, this does not alter the fact that it is their judgement which mainly determines the view on which society will act in the not too distant future.' Not once the process of comment and opinion forming is opened up to everyone.

For generations, this small elite used to decide what we heard, in what form we heard it and from what angle it was presented. They often decided too, who would be heard and who would not be heard. Not any longer, they don't – today everyone can be a broadcaster, and have a go at explaining, informing and analysing.

The internet pulverises monopolies and smashes hierarchy – not just in the world of business and commerce, but public life too. The elite – pundits, offi-cials, experts, scientists – who have exercised such a grip over the body politic of Western states for so long are losing their privilege status to guide and inform. The power of their prejudice in favour of doing things by grand design is on the wane.

The West will not just sound and feel a very differ-ent place. If we really are witnessing a decisive blow against top-down determinism – the death of what Hayek called 'constructive rationalism' – it will change the way the West is governed fundamentally.

A cultural revolution is coming that will unseat the constructivist elite that have presided over Western affairs for generations. The influence of the 'official mind' – bureaucrats, politicians, technocrats – who favour doing things by grand design will ebb away, while the power of the rest of us will grow.

The web is, by its very anarchic, decentralised, unplanned and hyper-networked nature, a repudiation of the notion that things are best done by design. It embodies the idea of spontaneous exchange and transaction. It hands the decisive advantage to those who hold that human affairs should best be ordered by the invisible hand of millions of individual transactions, rather than by top-down design.

I can already hear what was once dismissed as the voice of angry bloggers going mainstream; it was the elite who consistently favoured arranging society by deliberate design. Look where that took us? The subprime bubble. Bloated welfarism. Overseas aid that doesn't actually help poor people overseas. The euro disaster. Western profligacy.

The experts who have presided over Western decline will not only lose power. They will find it increasingly difficult to keep extorting wealth from the rest of us to finance their grand follies.

SMALL BECOMES BIG

Big used to be beautiful. News was broadcast to millions of people at the same time. Larger economies seemed more successful. Big states became great powers.

For much of the past two hundred years, everything seemed to be growing: the height of buildings, the span of bridges, the size of businesses. Modernity itself seemed at times to be about the march of mass production, mass consumption, mass markets.

The nineteenth and twentieth centuries saw ever greater mass production. Standardised goods and services were churned out, with competitive advantage going to producers that were able to leverage economies of scale.

In his book *The Long Tail*, Chris Anderson, editor-in-chief of *Wired* magazine, explains how this is starting to change. The internet pulverises monoliths and mass markets, and puts the emphasis on the niche.

Anderson begins with the examples of music and films. Until now, these industries were driven by the search for blockbusters. A new product had to attract a large number of purchasers in order to recoup its costs. A video, for example, needed to be rented with a certain frequency in order to justify the cost of the shelf space.

But the internet has abolished the need for shelf space. A film might be purchased online by only a handful of people; yet it still makes sense to offer the service, since doing so is effectively free. That is the 'long tail' of the title: all the ones and twos that are individually insignificant but that, in aggregate, represent considerable profit.

Generations of businessmen and women have known about the so-called 80/20 rule. This is a remarkably consistent ratio in business whereby approximately 20 per cent of the product range will account for 80 per cent of the sales – and, usually, 100 per cent of the profits.

Online retailing is turning the 80/20 assumption on its head. Anderson describes how again and again, online retailers offering mass inventories are discovering what he calls the '98 per cent rule' instead – which is that 98 per cent of inventory has at least one sale each quarter. In other words, instead of the lion's share of sales with 20 per cent of the inventory, in a world of unlimited choice, it is the aggregate market for all those niche sales that is really vast.

From a consumer's point of view, the tail represents a hitherto unimaginable extension of choice. A generation ago, teenagers listened to the music played by a handful of radio stations and watched whatever films were screened by their local cinema. Today, they have Amazon and iTunes and Rhapsody and Netflix and LoveFilm.

The internet not only allows niche markets to exist that were previously impossible, but niche production. And intriguingly, suggests Anderson, it will not only be niche markets in digital goods – MP3 files or films or books – but manufactured ones, too.

While we are some distance away from having consumer goods routinely made to order, technology means that the prospect of this happening no longer seems quite as remote as it once did. Already specialist dental and medical products are being made to order using additive manufacturing – or three-dimensional printing – technology. It is no longer impossible to imagine a world in which not only the books we buy on Amazon are printed on demand, but the new pair of spectacles or kitchen crockery are made on demand, too.

Perhaps one day mass production could even give way to personalised production, with digital technology and additive manufacturing allowing even complex items to be made to order for niche, highly personalised markets.

What we already know is that even today many

long-held assumptions about economies of scale are being turned on their head. Instead of profitability lying in bringing to market a million standardised products, the margins lie in enabling a million people to order a personalised product (think of Moonpig for greeting cards).

The internet is not only rewriting long-standing assumptions about business models and economies of scale. It is blurring all kinds of established boundaries.

Not only can we choose what we want to watch, we can increasingly *make* what we want – for another aspect of the long tail is that it breaks down the distinction between amateurs and professionals.

The internet, say some critics, is a job-destroying monster. Many of those things folk once paid for, they complain, we now expect to get for free – or for much less than before. This is, they claim, eroding profit margins, rendering business models redundant and destroying jobs.

Such claims are nonsense, made by dot com Luddites. Precisely the same complaints were made at the time of the industrial revolution – and no doubt at the time of the agricultural revolution, too.

The digital revolution is destroying jobs in the same way that the agrarian revolution destroyed careers in hunter-gathering. Or the industrial revolution destroyed jobs in weaving. Free from such occupations, people went on to produce wealth in other less arduous ways. Humankind grew more prosperous.

It is true that the internet allows us to have more for less – cheaper ebooks, cheaper flights and holidays, free newspapers online. But the agricultural and industrial revolution gave people more for less, too. Products that once took many hours of toil to produce were suddenly available at much lower cost to everyone. Food became more plentiful. Cloth and utensils became affordable. The internet will add to the productive capability of *Homo sapiens sapiens* even if Neanderthal pundits find this difficult to grasp.

The digital world blurs the distinctions between public and private.

An economist will tell you that a 'public good' is defined as a good whose enjoyment by one consumer does not diminish its availability for enjoyment by another. A good example of this might be, say, defence or law and order. So far, so good.

But isn't that conventional definition of a public good also a pretty good description of a lot of what you can buy online?

A newspaper might be printed off 200,000 or even half a million times each day. Every time someone bought a copy, they diminished the ability of everyone else to buy one. It was, your economist friend might say, a private good. But what happens when the newspaper is published online?

Even if you have to pay to read it online, like an awful lot of things available online, you can buy it without doing anything to diminish its availability to everyone else. So is it a private good, or does it became what we might call a 'club good' – somewhere in between? In other words, you can exclude others from enjoying it – a paywall – but their reading of the online version does nothing to diminish your enjoyment of it.

Suddenly a whole lot of private goods become a little more like public goods. And maybe a whole lot of goods that were that halfway house of 'club goods' become private goods. Digital technology allows you to encrypt TV signals all of a sudden.

At the same time, the internet is giving the private sphere some of what previously belonged to the public.

Take public data, for example. A lot of government departments in Britain make their data available publicly – albeit in a form that protects personal data. Data is streamed in 'mashable' form such that it can have private, as well as public, applications. Again, the boundary between what was the public and the private sphere might not be as clear cut as it was.

Or consider Google Maps, which millions of people now use to get around. Is it a public service? Of course Google Maps is provided by a private company. In that sense it is private. But it is ubiquitous and as much a social utility as any of the things that we accept as public services.

Perhaps our assumptions about what is public and what is private need to change – and the internet may be about to challenge many of our assumptions about public and private when it comes to politics and government, too.

SMALL-STATE ADVANTAGE
In the digital age, it pays to be small.

In the eighteenth century, Holland – once the leading power in Europe – was slowly eclipsed by larger England. During the nineteenth century, England was in turn overshadowed by much larger Germany, America and Russia. When it came to economic and military power, size, it seemed, used to matter.

So great were the advantages of being a big state, went the thinking for much of the twentieth century, that small states needed to be grouped together into regional trade blocs. Doing so, it was hoped, would give them the advantages of being big.

But today, one might instead ask, what is so great about being big?

Large countries are not more economically successful or prosperous. As Daniel Hannan puts it, 'if big really was beautiful, China would be more prosperous than Hong Kong, Indonesia than Brunei, France than Monaco and the EU than Switzerland.'[91]

Richest countries per capita.

Rank	Country	GDP per capita in $ (ppp)	Population (million)
1	Qatar	179,000	0.8
2	Liechtenstein	141,100	0.04
3	Luxembourg	82,600	0.5
4	Bermuda	69,900	0.07
5	Singapore	62,100	4.7
6	Jersey	57,000	0.09
7	Norway	54,600	4.7
8	Brunei	51,600	0.4
9	United Arab Emirates	49,600	5.1
10	Kuwait	48,900	2.6
11	United States	47,200	313.2
12	Andorra	46,700	0.08
13	Hong Kong	45,900	7.1
14	Guernsey	44,600	0.07
15	Cayman Islands	43,800	0.05
16	Gibraltar	43,000	0.02
17	Switzerland	42,600	7.6
18	Australia	41,000	21.8
19	Austria	40,400	8.2
20	Netherlands	40,300	16.8

Source: CIA Handbook

Indeed, the opposite is true. Smaller states prosper more than the large.

What do you notice about the list of richest countries on the planet? They are generally small. Only the United States (population 313 million) and Australia (22 million) are in any sense big.

'Ah! But they are all tax havens!' you say.

Some are. But how do you think they became tax havens? By having low taxes.

And what enabled these small-state tax havens to have lower taxes? Because they did not have the additional costs of being a big state, with a big government and a large administrative class demanding 40 per cent income taxes.

Small states generally have the advantage of smaller, more accountable government. Their elites tend not to be quite so remote. There are fewer quangos. Civil servants have less autonomy to do what suits them, rather than the electorate. There is less state apparatus able to start doing as it pleases.

There is, of course, one great exception on the list. The United States is eleventh richest in terms of per capita GDP, yet is a nation of 313 million people. Far from disproving the 'small is prosperous' rule, the United States rather reinforces it.

You see, America is a union, or federation, of lots of smaller states. It is precisely because it is a collection of smaller states that it has small-state advantage combined with what advantages there are in being big.

The age of the internet will bring even more advantages to smaller states, and even greater disadvantages to larger centralised blocs.

Most strikingly the internet has eliminated distance. Instead of having to be part of regional economies or trade groups, even the smallest country can be in close proximity to the whole world. Competition and capital are more mobile from every part of the planet than ever before.

Just as the internet gives advantages to small, nimble niche businesses, it allows smaller states to carve out a role and a market in the global economy.

THE iTAX BASE

What do politicians mean by the term 'tax base'?

The tax base are all those workers, consumers, businesswomen, entrepreneurs and others government taxes in order to do all the things that government tells us we need.

The very term tax *base* has connotations of solidity, reliability and dependability. The implication is that you can count on it being there.

The digital revolution will challenge this assumption. In a world where so much is just a mouse-click away, the tax base is about to look a whole lot less solid.

Here is a striking fact.

In 2010, US corporate profits were approximately $1.8 trillion. Adjusted for inflation, that meant US businesses were generating about twice as much profit in 2010 than they had been in the mid-1980s.

Yet the effective rate of taxation that US businesses were paying on those profits had fallen by over 40 per cent to 23 per cent.

How did this massive reduction in the rate of tax for US businesses happen?

Was it because successive administrations cut the

tax rates for businesses? Only in part. A one-off cut in the rate in the late 1980s does not alone explain the fall in the effective rate.

The reduction in the effective tax rates that US businesses pay is instead down to entirely legal tax minimisation practices, conducted on a massive scale.

Apple's federal tax bill in 2011, for example, is estimated to have been $2.4 billion lower than it might otherwise have been thanks to such tax minimisation tactics.[92]

It is not only America. Britain's largest online retailer, Amazon, generated £7.6 billion in sales between 2009 and 2012. What was the total corporation tax paid to the Treasury on that income? Nil.[93]

Is this shocking evidence of tax evasion and corporate wickedness on an industrial scale? There are plenty of government officials happy to think so. And plenty in the UK Uncut mob ready to shout about the need to 'make corporations pay'.

But what we are witnessing is not merely a matter of clever corporate tax lawyers exploiting tax loopholes. Something more profound is going on, which cannot be changed by closing a few supposed tax loopholes.

A generation or so ago, wealth was made when things were manufactured or mined. Of course, that still happens. But increasingly, in the modern economy, added value comes not merely from making things, but from the added intellectual value.

The high-value bit, to put it crudely, lies increasingly with the intellectual property rights.

Yet like all ideas, intellectual property is mobile. You might struggle to move a mining operation or a factory from one tax regime to another. But an idea can travel as swiftly as an email.

A great deal of so-called tax avoidance really boils down to a question of intellectual property: in which jurisdiction is this intellectual property taxable? Where is this intellectual property being exploited?

Instead of regarding what is happening as tax avoidance, perhaps we should see it as tax migration. Those who move intellectual property from one tax climate to another more benign one can no more be blamed for avoiding taxes than migrating birds can be blamed for avoiding winter. Only an oddball might hold it against them.

No wonder tax officials feel frustrated.

In Britain, Treasury officials would like to bring in a 'general anti-avoidance rule'. Instead of taxing businesses on the basis of pre-defined rules, specifying how much tax is payable and under what circumstances, this kind of arbitrary power would enable tax collectors to retrospectively bill businesses for what they think those firms ought to pay.

Perhaps this merely illustrates how no set of tax rules, however complex, can get to grips with the fact that the source of wealth in the modern world – intellectual property – can move.

Unless governments are prepared to adopt 1950s Albania-style isolationism, businesses will inevitably find it easier to transact business in a way that reduces their tax bill – and to do so quite legitimately.

And it will not simply be the giants who move. A generation ago, the largest gaming operator in my Essex constituency was, in my Essex constituency. Being a seaside town, the pier, with its amusement arcades and gaming, was an important part of the local economy, and one of the largest generators of public revenue.

Today, the largest gaming firms active in my Essex constituency are domiciled in Gibraltar. The amusement arcades are still there. The bingo hall is still there. But more folk place bets or play bingo online than visit either the amusement arcade or the bingo hall. And how do you tax that?

It is not just businesses. High net worth individuals can take flight too. With the top 1 per cent of the workforce paying 27 per cent of all the tax, you only need one in a hundred of the workforce to relocate to a different tax jurisdiction to lose a quarter of your tax revenue.

And even amongst the other 99 per cent, there simply are not the massed ranks of geese that there were a generation ago, waiting patiently in line to be plucked. Fifty years ago, big corporate businesses, employing tens of thousands of people, harvested enormous revenues for the government.

Back then, 'a typical firm was [...] a team of workers, hierarchically arranged and housed on a single site'. But increasingly wealth is created not by big corporate tax farms. Businesses are 'a nebulous and ephemeral coming together of creative and marketing talent to transmit the efforts of contracting individuals towards the satisfying of consumer preferences'.[94]

Half a century ago, Western economies were dominated by businesses like the Ford Motor Company or Bethlehem Steel. It was pretty easy to harvest income taxes from their hundreds of thousands of workers. You could even get their HR department to act as tax collector and send you the cheque.

But today eBay (market capitalisation $39 billion) and Google (market capitalisation $190 billion) have a greater value than Ford (market capitalisation $38 billion). Bethlehem Steel does not even exist.

In 1980, Ford had half a million employees in the US paying tax. Bethlehem Steel had 100,000 staff on the payroll. Today, Google has 16,800 employees, eBay 17,700.

Now do you see the trouble with the term tax *base*?

Back in 1966, 37 per cent of UK taxes came from taxes on incomes. Today, it is a mere 28 per cent, and the long-term trend is down.

In the United States in 2008, 36 per cent of taxes came from incomes, and in a mere two years it fell to 30 per cent.

Of course, the proportion of tax revenue from various sources bobs around a bit – but the long-term trend is away from taxes on incomes.

Over the next generation or so, this could have some fairly profound consequences. It will, perhaps, change the political economy of the West beyond recognition.

Taxes on income are, as we have seen, graduated. Whatever you think about the rights and wrongs of getting the wealthiest 10 per cent to pick up over half the bill, the point is that it can be done. Indeed, it has been under governments of all parties in almost every Western state for the past hundred or so years.

But how can you structure tax on consumption in the same way, so that the wealthier pay proportionately more? You can't. How can you get one in ten people to keep paying 50 to 60 per cent of the tax bill? You won't be able to.

Do you make someone pay a higher sales tax on the second DVD that they buy? Do you charge the millionaire, who fills up the tank with petrol more often, a higher amount of tax each time?

Such schemes would be unworkable. The reality is that if you tax people on consumption, you have to more or less charge a flat amount each time they consume. The more they consume, the more they pay.

In other words, taxes in the future will of necessity become much more proportional, and less graduated. The future is with flat taxes.[95]

Why does this matter?

As we saw in Chapter 2, the more unequal the tax rate, the more government can grow. And the more proportionate the tax rate becomes in the future, the less government there is going to have to be.

If you are taxing people on what they consume, it is no longer quite so easy to get 10 per cent of the population to pick up half the tax tab. You can no longer parcel out the costs of government unequally, and get folk to vote for the costs of more government, because they'll not get the bill.

As long as one in ten Americans pay most of the tax bill, and almost half of US households pay no federal income tax at all, low tax will be a more marginal issue. 100 per cent of American households are consumers, and would have to pay for any increase in tax on consumption. All of a sudden a lot more folk will develop an interest in lower taxes. The cost concealment that made Big Government possible is no longer possible the way it was.

➔

DIGITAL MONEY

It is not the moochers or the looters who give value to money.
Ayn Rand, *Atlas Shrugged*

Think back to when you last bought something online. What currency did you use?

This afternoon I was on Amazon buying Peppa Pig DVDs (for my two-year-old, I should add). I paid in pounds, I think. But I might have logged into the US version of the site, which lists prices in dollars. Or was it euros?

That is the thing about shopping online. You can pay for things priced in other currencies, with money from your bank account in something completely different. You do not even have to calculate the exchange rate, your bank does it for you.

Not so long ago, paying for things in cash using different currencies was a costly, time-consuming business. (Remember travellers' cheques?) Now we can do it at the click of a mouse and scarcely give it a second thought.

This ability for almost everyone to shop around online and use whatever currencies they like could have a profound impact on the way that we use and view money.

Britain has the pound, America the dollar, Europe the euro (for now), Japan the yen. We are so used to the idea of a money monopoly in each country that we do not really stop to question it.

But the digital revolution will turn our assumptions about money on their head.

In 2004, for the first time ever, there were more

electronic cash payments in Britain than actual cash payments. With more e-wallet technology on the way, it will become ever easier to pay for things in different currencies seamlessly.

The digital revolution is starting to allow us to make payments without banking. Instead of paying for things via banks – those vast, cumbersome institutions which require costly branches, bonuses and occasional bailouts – we will instead use mobile technology, or O2, Tesco or Bitcoin to pay for things. In parts of Africa, the M-Pesa system already sees millions of mobile-to-mobile payments being made without there being a Western-style bank branch network at all.

And once payments can be made using electronic phone credits or other e-currencies, where does 'official' money stop and a form of private or 'unofficial' currency start?

The idea of competing currencies might not be entirely new, but the internet – and the way that digital technology makes it possible to use different currencies seamlessly – is.

Digital technology gives us the ability to shop around using whatever currencies we like in a way that would have previously been impractical.

So what? Why does this matter?

As we saw in Chapter 2, since the collapse of the Bretton Woods currency system forty years ago, Western currencies have been run as fiat – or paper only – currencies. When it comes to managing the money supply, government has been the only constraint upon government. And, not surprisingly, government is not much good at reining in government.

Governments have tended to manage the money in their interests. As large debtors, with debts denominated in the currency they control, they have often been tempted to reduce their debt burden by debauching the value of the currency through inflation.

For four decades, almost every Western state has at some point attempted to inflate its way out of debt, and the currency deliberately debauched.

In 1971, when the United States broke the final link between the dollar and gold, it required $35 to buy one ounce of gold. You would need $1,590 to buy the same amount of gold today. Has gold really become more expensive? Perhaps a better way of looking at it is that with many, many more dollars in circulation now, each dollar has lost value.

As Philip Coggan puts it, 'the Romans took two hundred years to devalue their currency by that same amount ... our generation has achieved the trick in just forty years'.[96]

Government has debased the currency in order to enable officialdom to carry on living beyond its means – or, more accurately, the means of the rest of us to pay for it out of taxation. Manipulation of the money supply has enabled governments to spend without as much taxation as they would otherwise have required.

Without being able to debauch the currency, government would never have grown so big.

Currency competition could mean that the days when governments could manipulate the money at will are coming to a close.

If the George Osborne pound is the only currency choice citizens have, they are at the mercy of Mr Osborne. He – or the Bank of England officials to whom he foolishly defers – can carry on debauching the value of sterling to whittle away the size of the debts they have run up – ignoring the consequences for savers, shoppers or businesses.

But in a world of currency competition, those savers, shoppers and businesses can begin to escape the scam. And if millions of families and businesses start to use currencies that the Chancellor is not merrily debasing, it will make it harder for him to keep doing so. All of a sudden, another of those assumptions on which our Big Government model has been built starts to look a little wobbly.

Perhaps the last people to see any of this are those central bankers too busy manipulating the money. But sooner or later monetary policy will have to be run in to maintain a stable currency – not to transfer wealth from the private to the public sector in place of direct taxation.

For a generation or more, everyone has known that government needs to manage the money supply. All the wisest economists and Treasury officials agreed – even if they argued about how much money and credit government ought to put into the system. As if to prove how right all the right-thinking people were, the only folk who disagreed were an obscure group of so-called Austrian economists that no one took seriously.

The trouble is that 'everyone' – apart from those Austrian school cranks – failed to see the 2007 crunch coming.

What if the Austrian school economists turned out to be right all along? What if, as Ludwig von Mises put it, 'there is no means of avoiding the final collapse of a boom brought about by credit expansion. The alternative is only whether the crisis should come sooner as the result of a voluntary abandonment of further credit expansion, or later as a final and total catastrophe of the currency system involved'?[97]

For decades, the idea of a total currency catastrophe seemed absurd. Now look at Greece.

The crisis in the Eurozone is not simply a crisis for the euro. It is ominous for the future of fiat money.

For a decade or so, the European Central Bank accepted Greek, Spanish and Italian bonds as collateral.

It was the money-out-of-thin-air trick that allowed governments in Athens, Madrid and Rome to live beyond their means for years. It is the money-out-of-thin-air trick that has allowed governments in every Western capital to live beyond their means for years.

Those days are coming to an end – and not only on the periphery of the Eurozone.

Von Mises's term 'further credit expansion' is a pretty good description of the print-more-money-and-pray approach taken by the US and the UK governments in response to the credit crunch. It has not fixed the problem, and both governments have had to keep on pumping ever larger doses of cheap money and credit into the system to stop it disintegrating.

Each time they do so, they make it more – not less – likely that their citizens and savers will begin using some other currency in time.

The sheer size of Western debts makes it very likely that governments will continue to debauch the currency. In doing so, government monopoly money will start to resemble monopoly money in every sense of the term.

Perhaps the digital revolution will not only give people alternative means of paying for things, one of a currency's key functions. Perhaps it will give rise to alternative methods for storing wealth. Governments have historically given themselves the right to decide what is and what is not money. Perhaps one of the consequences of manipulating the money is that governments will find that they lose this right. In Zimbabwe, folk now use US dollars. It just sort of happened. Who is to stop those living in Athens from switching to some other currency, too?

It is easy to forget, but the West has had a system of paper currency controlled by politicians and officials for a mere forty-one years. Until 1914, the world's currency system – the classic gold standard – was a product not of deliberate design, but of accident and imitation. Even after the end of the classic gold standard, pegs to gold, or to currencies pegged to gold, constrained how much money governments produced until 1971. Only since 1971 have Western politicians been free to manipulate the money at will.

Perhaps it is this notion of 'currency by design', controlled by politicians and central bankers, that will prove to be an aberration.

That is the thing about organic, Hayekian design. You cannot be sure what designs will emerge. One thing we can be certain of is that the digital revolution is making the world more Hayekian, and not only when it comes to the currency.

❯

Each of the three great technological revolutions – the agrarian, the industrial and now the digital – has transformed, or will transform, the way that human societies are organised.

The farming revolution allowed humans to live a settled existence, first on farms, then in villages and small towns. The industrial revolution enabled towns to grow into much larger cities. It also enabled the emergence of the bureaucratic, centralised state.

The digital revolution – which is only just beginning – will mean hyper-personalisation, and less deference to the experts. Instead of leaving it to an elite to make generic choices for the rest of us, we will decide things for ourselves – including what opinions we hold.

Intellectually, it will become much harder to justify seeking to arrange human affairs on the basis of grand design. Financially, it will be much harder to pay for it. Unable to manipulate the money or count on a solid tax base, the old bureaucratic state will become progressively more unaffordable.

Politics – so long the process for making and imposing one-size-fits-all choices – is starting to change, too.

iPOLITICS

Old-school politics is dead. There are still plenty of elections. It is simply that those whom voters put in office no longer really determine public policy when they get there.

Officialdom has grown too big, technocrats have gained too much autonomy. Public policy is made in the interests not of the public, but of a remote elite, prone to fads and dogma.

The governing and the governed have grown detached.

The digital revolution is about to close the gap. It will breathe new life into a very different kind of politics. It will galvanise the actual public – not merely those who preside in their name. It will enable ordinary people to apply real pressure on those who today only notionally represent them. It will restore purpose to our supine legislatures, and lead to a new kind of democracy.

THE WAY THINGS WERE

Just over a hundred years ago, in 1910, there was a parliamentary election in my Essex constituency. The winner, a Mr Harry Newton, won with 6,470 out of

11,478 votes cast. A century later, I was elected MP for the same seat with 22,867 votes out of 43,123 votes cast.

I point this out not to boast, but to show that to get elected to the House of Commons in 1910, you needed many fewer votes – and the backing of many fewer individual voters. In fact, you could probably, at a push, make a good go of getting to meet most of the elector-ate personally. You could certainly fit a sizeable chunk of them into town hall meetings.

And that is precisely what used to happen. Come polling day, the voters then made a choice about you – the person – not just the party under whose banner you stood.

Pretty soon after 1910, the electorate grew dramati-cally. Women were given the vote a few years later. Then younger people. The population rose. This all transformed the way that we did politics locally – and nationally.

With an increase in the number of voters, the kind of familiarity between voters and candidates that existed previously was impossible. By the 1990s, voters might even struggle to know the name of the candidates, let alone know what they stood for.

In 1910, a candidate speaking in town hall meet-ings, or standing in the market square, could get their message out to the few thousand supporters they needed directly. By the mid-1990s, candidates might still loiter around market squares, but most politi-cal communication was conducted not by individual candidates appealing to voters directly, but by party machines through the mass media.

Thanks to mass media and a greater mass of voters, the business of politics became much more of a choice between parties, rather than personalities. It has become much more impersonal, and much more of a contest between generic brands. Indeed, until 1969, it was expressly forbidden for a candidate standing in a parliamentary election to give any indication of his or her party affiliation on the ballot paper. Election law itself expected you to vote for the person, not the party.[98]

By the 1990s, many voters would have struggled to know where to mark their ballot paper without being able to see the party affiliations of the different candidates.

This made politicians seem more remote and less accountable to those they serve.

With radio, newspapers and television carrying their message for them, political parties put more effort into trying to get their message out via broadcasters, rather than directly. They tried to control the message, with candidates given 'lines to take' to parrot dutifully.

Nor did this end once a candidate was elected to Parliament. In Britain, MPs were – until very recently – fed 'lines to take' on a daily basis. Because politicians were communicating via the mass media, they increasingly did so using duplicate slogans and clichés. Small surprise that they started to sound and feel like a caste apart.

As politics became a mass brand business, political parties began to control the message, gaining much greater power. Politics became centralised.

But the generic brand approach to politics was increasingly unable to cater for different tastes. The generic brands started to lose market share.

In 1950, almost 90 per cent of voters supported either the Conservatives or Labour. In 2010, a mere 65 per cent did. Big established political parties have been steadily losing market share to the niche, to the United Kingdom Independence Party, the Greens, the Welsh and Scottish Nationalists. There is good evidence that within the established parties, local candidates with a strong distinctive, local brand tend to perform better on polling day than candidates that recycle the generic script.

In an age of generic brand politics, the voters increasingly seem to have an appetite for the something a little more niche and authentic.

In most continental European democracies, the 'party list' system has meant an even greater degree of centralisation. Voters are not even able to vote for a specific candidate at all, but forced to vote for the brand. Parties are then allocated seats depending on what share of the votes they got. Candidates are then allocated a place in the legislature depending on how slavishly loyal they are to the party hierarchy.

In Europe, established political parties have lost market share to some altogether less benign new entrants; in France the Front National regularly polls over 15 per cent and the Vlaams Belang 20 in Belgium.

In contrast, American politics has several key features specifically designed to prevent law makers becoming remote: candidates are selected via open primaries; there are term limits and recall procedures to control politicians; mechanisms exist to allow local and state-wide referendums.

Founded in popular revolt against an autocratic government, US politics is built on what one might term Jeffersonian ideals: the notion that decisions should be taken as closely as possible to the people they affect.

Yet even in America, politics has been increasingly centralised. It was in America that mass brand party politics was pioneered. It was US politicians who invented the notion of 'spin' and of 'triangulation': using the message to manipulate voter opinion. And popular disdain for those inside the remote 'beltway' is perhaps as great in America as it is in any other democracy.

As politics has grown more centralised, and more impersonal, elected law makers are perhaps no longer directly responsible for fulfilling their promises the way they once were. When Harry Newton issued an election address to the local electorate in 1910, it was his personal pledge. Yet for most of the past century, elected law makers have been representatives of the party in their constituency, rather than of their constituents in the legislature.

This perhaps helps explain why once fiercely independent legislatures have been willing to gradually surrender many of their powers in the first place. If Parliament no longer answered quite so directly to the people, government no longer answered so directly to Parliament. Parliaments and assemblies have grown supine because their members are not in close proximity to those who elect them. Mass brand democracy has insulated them. They are not under such a piercing spotlight. It is their party – for which they are just a spokesman – that is held responsible.

This makes it far easier for politicians to delegate decisions. If the voters are not constantly on your back, why jump on the back of the civil servants?

It is often claimed that politicians in Britain farm out responsibility to quangos and officials out of fear

– in order to pass on responsibility to someone else. I suspect that the real reason they delegate so much autonomy to unelected officials is because they feel they are in closer proximity to the technocratic class in SW1 than they are to the hoi polloi outside. No matter which party or which constituency they are elected from, they feel more on the side of the governing class in Westminster than what they regard as the unforgiving mob outside.

It seems so sensible to leave those tricky decisions to the disinterested experts, to those urbane, Oxbridge-educated experts. I suspect that Merovingian kings decided to leave more and more of the detail to their court stewards for much the same sort of reason.

iPOLITICS

The internet is breathing new life into politics – but it is a very different beast that will spring to life.

Politics is being repersonalised.

Of course, when voting for a US President, voters have never stopped voting for the person, rather than the party. Ask most Americans for whom they voted in 2008 or 1980, and they are likely to say Obama or Reagan. But for much of the past century, voters elected law makers on the basis of the generic party brand, rather than the calibre of the individual candidates.

You can see why. There simply was not the channel for direct communication between candidates and voters to allow voters to make that kind of choice.

Candidates standing for Parliament in Harwich in 1987 or 1997 simply did not have the means to communicate with thousands of voters directly and personally, the way email, YouTube, Twitter and Facebook enable me to do today.

Rather than try to coax and encourage a news editor to carry the message I want to the voter, I am able to cut out the middle man and the medium, and communicate directly. And the communication becomes a two-way process. The internet allows the voter to put direct questions and pressure on law makers.

This niche, direct communication enables voters to do something they've been unable to do for generations: make a choice of whom to vote for in terms of the personality and calibre of the candidate, rather than the quality of the party brand.

Thanks to the internet, politics is no longer simply about pushing out generic messages. There is suddenly scope for that which is distinctive, niche, particular and local. More and more politicians – even under the umbrella of the generic party brands – are starting to carve out their own identities.

Or as George Galloway, winner of the Bradford West by-election, put it after his crushing victory as a Respect party candidate, 'our media was social media ... Twitter, Facebook and YouTube ... at the touch of a button, I can speak to thousands of people ... Our election campaign was built entirely outside the Westminster bubble.'[99]

Digital communication not only brings the politician closer to the voter, it brings the voter up close and personal to the politician. And this means political hyper-accountability.

Instead of taking at face value what politicians say that they said and voted for, we can check. We do not need to rely on the opinion of a newspaper reporter – who probably drinks in the same bar and eats in the same taxpayer-subsidised restaurant in Westminster or Washington – to tell us either.

It's not just how politicians do their politics that is open to accountability. They can be held to account for how they behave, too.

In Britain, the MPs' expenses scandal saw dozens of politicians, who had used taxpayer-funded expense accounts to pay for lavish lifestyles, turfed out of office. The public only got to know the detail of how their representatives had been spending taxpayer money because disks containing the data had been leaked to a national newspaper. But pre-digital, the sheer volume of information would have made it impossible to leak in that way – or then be scrutinised and assessed the way it was.

The internet means politicians are under the micro-scope as never before. They cannot hide behind blanket generic messages as they used to. They are held directly accountable by the folk back home, who decide if they get turfed out of office or not. The folk out there – in the world beyond the beltway and Westminster – are now just a mouse-click away from you, and they want more from you than the generic party line.

Politicians are all of a sudden much more outwardly accountable than they have ever been, and less inward looking.

Closer proximity to the voter means that law makers are increasingly inclined to side with the voter, rather than simply represent the party line to them. They are, if you like, starting to change sides.

Or perhaps, one ought to say, to return to their side.

In Britain, until the First World War, a Member of Parliament elected as a backbencher, but invited to

join the government, was required to resign from the
House of Commons, and stand for re-election in a
by-election.

Why? Because the MP was seen to be changing sides.
Having been elected by the people to hold government
to account, they were joining it – and needed to renew
their mandate from the voters before doing so.

In the United States, where the principle of
the separation of powers was enshrined in the
Constitution, members of the legislature have always
kept greater distance from the executive. But they
have not always been seen to be on the side of those
outside the beltway.

Once again, elected representatives are starting to
side with those who sent them to Westminster and
Washington, rather than the party hierarchy that they
find there.

This is not happening because politicians somehow
'get' the internet – although some do. They are recon-
necting with voters less because they see the light, and
more because they are beginning to feel the heat.

When dozens of the governing Conservative Party's
MPs recently defied their party leadership to vote in
favour of a referendum on Britain's EU membership,
they were not part of a Westminster plot or conspiracy.
Rather they were each individually responding to
intense pressure put on them by a network of voters
who decided that they wanted their politicians to
honour what they regarded as a pre-election promise.

This is, opine the Westminster pundits, the most
rebellious Parliament in recent British history.[100] If the
pundits had the measure of the changes that the web
is bringing to politics, they would not be surprised by

what is greater responsiveness by the elected to those who elected them. If the pundits properly understood this, they might even stop referring to law makers who stood up for the interests of their voters as 'rebels'.

The internet means that voters want more from their representative than a taxpayer-funded mouthpiece for the government machine. And we are consequently starting to see changes in Congress and Parliament.

The House of Commons is starting to get off its knees. After decades of meekly accepting how government controls Parliament, Parliament is starting to claw back control over government.

It started small. Commons rules were changed to give MPs, not government whips, the power to decide who gets to be the Commons Speaker. And guess what? They elected as Speaker someone called John Bercow, previously most famous for getting up the nose of old-school party bosses.

Then they started to demand that the man they put in the Speaker's chair favour not one side or party over another, but the interests of the legislature over the executive. Ministers are now summoned to appear before the Commons three or four times a week, whereas before a minister would be unlikely to face such a summons over the entire course of a five-year parliament.

Then MPs demanded the power to hold properly competitive elections for committee chairmanships. They won, turfing out many of the government's pet placemen who had previously filled such posts. Perhaps all this insider stuff passed you by.

Maybe you started to notice something was up when these committees got all aggressive and summoned ministers, and then media moguls, to appear before them. The legal summons instructing the Murdochs to appear before the Commons had not previously been issued within living memory.

Once a sheep, full of wannabe ministers, Parliament has started to grow some fangs.

Those we elect have begun to hold government to account in a way they failed to do for generations. MPs are now even agitating to make all executive appointments subject to confirmation hearings – with some MPs also demanding the right to veto departmental spending and fire ministers.

Little in terms of outward appearance has changed, yet at the heart of Britain's system of parliamentary democracy subtle, yet profound, changes are afoot. Government no longer controls Parliament the way it did for most of the past century. Increasingly Parliament – and the people – are beginning to control government.

Where did this change of heart come from? From below. Years of deferential democracy in Britain have evaporated in the digital age. The MPs' expenses scandal destroyed forever the idea that 650 politicians will make the right choices if left to themselves. With the internet, MPs are no longer left to get on with the business of politics. No longer insulated from the people, politicians are starting to take note of them, not just the party whips in Westminster. Politics is opening up to everyone, not just the Westminster club.

When members of Congress decided to approve the Obama bailout package, despite having indicated to their electorates that they would not, they were taken to task by voters.

Utah Senator Robert Bennett, a three-term incumbent, lost the Republican Party nomination in 2010 after he voted to support the bank bailout. The same fate befell Senator Arlen Specter after thirty years in the job. And Bob Inglis. And Parker Griffith.

The Tea Party movement is an expression of frustration with generic 'politics as usual'. But it is more than that. A grass-roots movement set up through the internet, it is also a way of doing politics outside party structures – and perhaps even without parties. There may or may not be a future in the Tea Party. I suspect that there is a big future in politics without hierarchical parties.

It is not only on the centre right that such groups are mobilising. New organisations are springing up across the political spectrum demanding accountability from politicians, including 38 Degrees and MoveOn.org.

Politics will increasingly be shaped by groups of like-minded people, mobilising online and pressurising their representatives. Online pressure from outside Washington and Westminster won't just help politicians decide what to do. It will also help decide what happens to politicians.

While voters used to decide who got elected to Congress or Parliament, it was political insiders who tended to decide how a politician's career went once they got there.

A Congressman or MP with a massive majority endorsing his or her views might cut a marginal, eccentric figure once they got to Washington or Westminster precisely because they held such views. An aristocracy of media pundits and party bosses tended to set the 'share price' of different law makers – and the need to cultivate this clique of insiders tended to make the more ambitious politicians answer to those inside the beltway or SW1.

Outspoken candidates for office might suddenly trim their views once they got to Washington. Instead of speaking out on the issues that counted in the constituency, MPs suddenly ditched views that might mark them out as a crank within the Westminster village. The pressure to conform once elected tempered the views and voting behaviour of all but the mad and the bad.

But this, too, is changing.

Already we have seen how the internet enabled a politician to come from the outside, appealing directly to voters over the heads of the party bigwigs. The phenomenon began with Howard Dean, a candidate for the Democratic nomination in 2004. Dean, who based his appeal on an angry and populist opposition to the Iraq War, was heartily disliked by most senior Democrats. Lacking the support of a party machine and of the big financial donors, he looked like being one of the many minnows who contest the early primaries before dropping out. But something surprising happened: the internet allowed him to mobilise a nationwide regiment of foot soldiers and small donors.

Dean ran his party close, but in the end came second. Not so the new boy, Senator Barack Obama in 2008. Less of an outsider than Dean, Obama was nonetheless written off before the primaries began. The Clinton clique's hold on party structures and financial muscle would be insuperable, ran the conventional wisdom.

In the event, Obama managed to raise millions in small donations, appealing directly to the electorate outside the Democratic Party. That appeal – or rather

Obama's ability to realise his appeal through the web – was the basis of his victory in the Democratic primaries.

Nothing, however, compares with the phenomenon of Ron Paul, the libertarian Republican, who on December 16 2007, broke all records by raising over $6 million from 37,000 online donors in a single day.

Candidates do not come bigger as outsiders than Paul. He was considered a maverick almost to the point of lunacy. But he is perhaps the first example of a politician whose appeal was created online. Not only did he outperform his rivals in internet donations; he also tended to come top in online polls. Although his views were not shared by most voters, they turned out not to be quite as way out as the pundits had assumed. To put it another way, a small group of political professionals – pundits, pollsters, party grandees – no longer decides who is mainstream and who is eccentric.

Before the internet, whatever a minister might have announced was intrinsically newsworthy. The very fact of holding ministerial office guaranteed the attention of the handful of political correspondents who controlled the news monopoly. It was an age of 'spin', when a few dozen party PR people and broadcasters could decide what the political narrative was.

Today politics is covered by hundreds of bloggers and amateurs. Lobby correspondents have competition from those whose views and analysis can be heard, too. A politician must now compel attention by virtue of what he is saying, rather than the position he occupies.

Suddenly what a politician says and does is no longer assessed through the filter of insider pundits. It is gauged by the crowd on the blogs. It is filtered by those

a long way from the bars and dining rooms of the capital. What might seem unthinkable to those who have
spent half a lifetime in Westminster or on Capitol Hill
is being thought, debated and urged by those outside.

THE RISE OF THE CITIZEN-CONSUMER

'Here comes everybody,' said Clay Shirky. And the
internet is bringing everybody into politics, too. We are
no longer leaving politics up to the whips, lobbyists,
pundits and think-tankers.

It is not that there is now a 'digital *demos*', a small
group of nerds, geeks and online obsessives – although
there are plenty of those. Rather it is that the *demos* is
now online.

In the twenty first century, democracy will be
shaped by this citizen-consumer interest much the
way twentieth-century democracy was shaped by
the interests of organised labour.

The coming of railways and trade unions in the late
nineteenth century saw the rise of organised labour.
Never just about better wages and working conditions,
organised labour had a profound impact on politics.

The rise of organised labour forced the established
parties in Britain to merge in the 1920s. From Australia
to Norway to Israel, parties founded by the interests
of organised labour held office for much of the past
century. In the United States, the Democratic Party
became the party of organised labour, with formal
union affiliation.

The rise of organised labour not only changed the
party political landscape. It shifted the political centre
of gravity. Politics in most Western democracies
became a contest between the interests of organised

labour versus the rest, a debate about the extent to which the architecture of the state should be shaped in the labour interest.

Imagine if broadband allows citizen-consumers to do what railways allowed organised labour to once do. Imagine if the *demos* online starts to mould democracy the way the trade union movement once did.

Citizen-consumers take it for granted that they can make their own choices and selections when it comes to what music they listen to, or what products they buy. If political parties want them to buy into their political offerings, they will have to allow citizen-consumers to help select party candidates.

The United States has a long-established tradition of primary and caucus selection. The internet means that these contests have become ever more open and unpredictable.

In Britain, where it has become the norm for parties to impose lists of candidates on local party branches, political parties have started to choose parliamentary candidates via both open primaries and caucuses. From November 2012, there will be local ballots held throughout most of England to elect a local police chief for each police force (except London), and a number of political parties are using open selection methods to ensure that everyone – not just party members – has a say. A number of parties may of course continue to select candidates for office using the old system, but they will probably lose market share as a result.

As politics becomes more 'open source', parties will themselves become less hierarchical. Those that run for office will have a longer leash, and greater auton-omy. The internet gives us unprecedented choice. It

smashes hierarchy and breaks open concentrations
of power. It strips away barriers to entry, allowing in
nimble upstarts. It forces established players to either
adapt or lose market share.

Those, at least, are some of the things it has done to
the world of business and commerce. It is about to do
much the same to the world of party politics.

Citizen-consumers will not only want more choice
and selection when it comes to choosing party
candidates, or voting for candidates with their own
distinctive appeal. They will also want to make more
political decisions for themselves.

The internet allows people to group together online
and apply pressure directly. Voters are able to press
their judgement upon individual Congressmen and
women. But they are able to demand the right to make
more choices directly.

We will see more direct democracy, where voters are
able to initiate debates and votes on what matters to
them. Just as they decide what is on their MP3 player,
so too will they have a role in programming the legislative agenda.

Already in Britain a new system of ePetitions is allowing the *demos* to force votes – and put on to the agenda
items that perhaps their representatives cannot, or will
not, address. Why leave it to a distant DJ to select the
music when you can help choose the playlist?

Perhaps most significant of all, the citizen-consumer
might not necessarily want the power to vote or make
one-size-for-everyone choices at all. Instead, as we
shall see in the next chapter, the citizen-consumer will
demand in the public sphere the same freedom to exer-
cise individual choices that he or she already takes for

granted in the private. If organised labour shifted the boundary between the public and the private in favour of the former, the citizen-consumer may well shift it back in favour of the latter.

EDMUND BURKE DOT COM

'But', claim the old guard, 'this direct democracy thing is not really what politics is supposed to be about. Deciding things is what we politicians are for – not the people.'

Often when a politician recycles some common-place thought, but thinks that what they have said is original and clever, they speak, I cannot help notice, with a slightly superior smile.

Many a time have I listened to MPs wearing such a smirk as they invoke the great eighteenth-century statesman Edmund Burke, in defence of the notion that politics be left to the politicians.

Why? Because Burke's famous 1774 address to the Bristol electorate is, on the face of it, a magnificent defence of the idea that those we elect should exer-cise their own judgement, not slavishly transpose the wishes of those who elected them.

An elected representative, said Burke, ought to 'live in the strictest union ... and the closest correspond-ence' with his constituents. 'Their wishes ought to have great weight with him; their opinion, high respect; their business, unremitted attention. It is his duty to sacrifice his repose, his pleasures, his satisfactions, to theirs; and above all, ever, and in all cases, to prefer their interest to his own.'

'But', Burke went on, your MP's 'unbiased opinion, his mature judgment, his enlightened conscience, he ought not to sacrifice to you, to any man, or to any set of men living ... Your representative owes you ... his judgment; and he betrays, instead of serving you, if he sacrifices it to your opinion.' So there, Burke seemed to be saying. He knew best, not the people.

So there, today's defenders of deferential democracy seem to say by invoking Burke. Even the great Edmund Burke says it is so, so it must be.

There is one slight problem with citing Burke's 238-year-old defence of the right of MPs to ignore the wishes of their electorate: not long after hearing what Burke had to say, the Bristol electorate threw him out of office. Far from being an advertisement for ignoring the wishes of the people, what happened to Burke ought to serve as a warning.

If one studies what Burke said in a little more detail, his main justification for trusting his judgement, rather than that of the electorate living in Bristol, was that those in Bristol were some 'three hundred miles distant from those who hear the arguments'.

It is an argument that was a little easier to make in 1774. Before people had radios, television, 24-hour news or the internet, folk living in Bristol might well have found it hard to follow debates taking place in the Palace of Westminster. Could such a point be made today?

Back in the days when the fastest thing in the country was a horse, politics had to be left to politicians. You had no choice but to send your representatives to far-away palaces by the Thames or the domed capitol on the Potomac, and have them decide things.

Today we no longer need to leave it to politicians in distant assemblies to decide things that we are able to decide for ourselves. Invoking Edmund Burke is not enough to hold back the pressure for more direct democracy.

THE NEW CENTRE OF POLITICAL GRAVITY

The rise of the citizen-consumer will shift the centre of political gravity, just as the rise of organised labour in the late nineteenth century did. It will realign politics neither to the left nor to the right, but instead pull it down from the elites to the people.

As it does so, politics will become more liberal – in the classical English sense of the word – and more libertarian.

Edmund Burke was sceptical about democracy because he feared – as many do today – that the common people had dangerous and angry passions. Mass democracy, it was feared, would become demagoguery. Unpopular minorities would be subject to the arbitrary rule of the mob.

In fact the evidence is that the precise opposite is happening. iDemocracy is leading to smaller, less arbitrary government.

In 2010, the UK government introduced a system of ePetitions. This allows campaigners, citizens and pressure groups to initiate debates and votes in the House of Commons.

Just as Burke might have done, the political punditry in our own time warned of the dark consequences of letting the mob decide. The BBC reported the ePetitions innovation entirely in terms of them being a vehicle that might allow the restoration of capital punishment.

But one year on, let's have a look at which ePetitions actually attracted the most popular support.

ePETITIONS RESULTS: NUMBER OF BACKERS

1. Convicted rioters to lose benefits – 217,921
2. Disclosure of all government documents relating to 1989 Hillsborough disaster – 109,482
3. Cheaper petrol and diesel – 60,045
4. Make financial education a compulsory part of the school curriculum – 40,069
5. Retain the ban on capital punishment – 24,822
6. Keep Formula 1 free to air in the UK – 21,301
7. Referendum on EU membership – 21,252
8. Restore capital punishment – 16,996
9. Public & private pension increases – change from RPI to CPI – 16,756
10. Increase policing – 9,366

(Source: Cabinet Office ePetitions site, 2011)

Far from mob rule, the top petition is demanding that the government take on the mobs. After an outbreak of mass looting and lawlessness over the summer of 2011, perhaps not surprisingly the petition with the most signatures demanded that the state withhold benefits from looters. Draconian and demagogic? Hardly. People simply want proper accountability before officials dole out public money.

The second most popular proposal – that the government release data on the Hillsborough disaster – is a demand for more open and accountable government. Not much arbitrary or draconian to be found in popular tastes there.

The third most popular demand? That the government take less money from our pockets each time we fill up the car.

What about the fear that ePetitions would lead to the restoration of the death sentence?

Look at what has actually happened. The ePetition demanding we maintain the ban on capital punishment came in at no. 5, beating the proposal that the death penalty be restored, down at no. 8.

Far from demanding the persecution of minorities, one proposal wants to change the way state pensions are calculated to help older folk. Only one proposal – financial education – is about any form of compulsion.

According to the text books, liberal democracies can either be more democratic or more liberal. The more powerful the interests of the *demos*, the more arbitrary and illiberal government becomes. The text books will need to be rewritten.

The more powerful citizen-consumers become, the more they will demand open and accountable government. The less arbitrary and remote officialdom will become.

Citizen-consumers will, of course, be consumers. Like all consumers, they will be keen to make discerning judgements about the quality of the goods and services that they get in return for the money that they spend. Citizen-consumers will want to make discerning judgements about the value of what they get not only as private citizens, but as taxpaying consumers of public services, too.

Today, the biggest purchase that citizen-consumers make during their lives is the bill they pay for government. As we saw in Chapter 1, for every $100 that the average American worker earns, $36 is spent on buying government. In Britain, the average worker buys £46 of government for every £100 earned. In Japan, the average worker spends ¥33 of every ¥100 earned. In France and Germany, amazingly, after spending €59 paying for government, the average worker has only €41 of what they earn to spend on themselves directly.

The citizen-consumer is going to start making some pretty discerning judgements about the value that he or she is getting back for all that.

As the tax burden shifts, as in this digital age it must, away from taxes on income towards taxes on consumption and property, those keen on lower taxes will no longer be a marginal force in politics. They will dominate it in a way they have been unable to since the introduction of graduated income tax almost a century ago.

Today one in ten voters picks up over half the income tax bill. But every citizen is a consumer. Once you start taxing people on the basis of what they consume, rather than what they earn, you have many more citizens intent on keeping taxes down.

CHAPTER 10

THE iSTATE

Remember your old PC? From the moment you took it out of the box and booted it up, to the time you threw it away, it had the same standardised software.

Twentieth-century governments were a bit like that. Every few years a new one came along with the same standardised software applications. And once you had it installed, you had to make do with what it could do for you, or wait for another one.

Today, of course, laptops and iPads are designed for you to download the kind of software or apps that you want. In the same way, more and more of the things that we get from government will be things that we choose to download for ourselves.

Each year we each get sent a tax bill – or at least the six in ten of us who pay income tax do. The bureaucratic state just about manages to retain a record of what it thinks we each owe it.

The iState won't just keep a personalised account of what we pay to it, but of what it owes us. As citizen-consumers, it will be up to us to use what the iState credits us with to buy many of the bits of government that we need – just as an iPad owner builds their own personalised library of apps. Government will be increasingly self-selected by us as citizens, not dished out to us as subjects.

Each year in the United States, government buys $24,268 of public services for every adult American. In Britain, the government buys $20,208 of services per adult, in Japan the figure is $15,586 and in France $23,635. Even if we were only able to self-select a third, or even a quarter of the services government provides us with, that is going to mean a lot of self-commissioning.

The digital revolution makes the iState feasible. The rise of the citizen-consumer makes it desirable. Looming public finance disaster makes it unavoidable.

THE GREAT EXPECTATIONS GAP

Never has the expectations gap been so wide. When we book a holiday or download a film we expect choice and immediacy. We browse the internet for options, we click a couple of buttons, and we get what we came for.

Compare this to the experience of applying for a passport, or getting planning permission – or trying to get your child into a particular school.

The mismatch between what we experience as consumers with what we have to put up with as citizens is not just confined to what happens online. We have unprecedented choice over most aspects of our lives. Our niche tastes are catered for when we buy coffee – 'Decaf skinny latte with cream'. Or when we buy a car – 'Diesel model with sat nav and headrest screens fitted'.

Yet when it comes to what we get from government, too often we have to make do with what we are given.

Consumers are empowered as never before – except in their dealings with the state. Previous generations were much readier to accept that what they wanted might not be on offer, and that even when it was, they might have to queue for it. But the internet has created almost unlimited choice, eliminating storage costs and reducing barriers to entry.

Whatever we want, the chances are that someone somewhere will be selling it. And it is now more feasible than ever to deal with that someone – unless that someone happens to be a government agency.

The mismatch between state provision and private sector provision is not a new phenomenon; the free market has always tended, on average, to deliver more efficient outcomes than government departments.

Governments tend to be, by their very nature, monopolies, less prone to competition. Government agencies more often answer to other bits of government for their budgets, rather than fee-paying customers. Services provided by the state have long been of inferior quality to those that could be provided privately.

None of this is new. What is different is the extent of the disparity between our experience as citizens in our dealing with government, and our experience as consumers dealing with everything else.

The gap between what we experience as customers and as citizens is becoming a chasm. An ever wider range of goods and services are produced and distributed to us as individuals, in accordance with our own circumstances and preferences. Except the things provided for us by government.

WHY GOVERNMENT CANNOT GIVE US CHOICE

'But democracy does give us choice,' you venture.

Of course. It lets voters choose between candidates

for office. But what else does it actually allow the *demos* to decide?

Even if those we elect to office were to actually formulate public policy, instead of leaving it to the battalions of officials who usually decide things, how would voting actually change things for you?

Politics in most Western states tends to boil down to a binary choice: Labour or Conservative, Democrat or Republican, Gaullist or Socialist. At a push, it might be a two-and-a-half-horse race – the Liberal Democrats in Britain, some sort of Ross Perot independent in America.

So you vote for whichever one of the two and a half brands you think is on balance more competent. Or has a broad approach that you agree with. Or maybe they said something that vaguely sounded like what you want. Or because the other lot repel you.

But how does any of that translate into deciding anything specific to you?

Perhaps one of the candidates happened to say something about the importance of children learn- ing via synthetic phonics, and as a parent you happen to agree. But even if that were so, it is a remarkably roundabout way to get your child the education they want. More likely placing your 'X' on the ballot paper next to their name won't change the way your child is taught the next day, if at all.

And what if you want your kid to study Spanish, rather than French – or do some extra maths? The chances of any of the candidates or parties offering that sort of detail in a manifesto are pretty small. So the binary choice you make on polling day is hardly likely to deliver any of that.

Binary ballot choices – even for local town hall elections – are simply too crude a method for determining
those kinds of things. Your vote – along with everyone
else's – might at best decide which side gets in, and the
broader approach they take to the macro questions of
the day. But it does not really give you direct choice
over the bits of government that preside over your
micro world.

Or as Arthur Seldon put it, the idea that elections
mean that we get 'services for "the good of the people",
where people can have services that suit their diverse
preferences and circumstances, is a fiction'.

Imagine if every household in your street decided
what breakfast cereal everyone should eat for the next
four or five years by holding a ballot. You would all get
to vote for your favourite. Suppose that 45 per cent
opted for cornflakes and 40 per cent Weetabix. Muesli,
Cheerios and Grape Nuts would make up the 'also rans'
on less than 1 per cent each in the polls.

Would everyone in the street where you live be satisfied with four or five years of cornflakes? Of course not.
The idea of collectively voting to decide the way that we
should each spend a few dollars or pounds on cereals
would be absurd. So why is it right to use such a system
to make even more important choices, involving even
larger sums?

Yet that is the logic for so much government.

Instead of ballot box elections to decide who eats what
cereal, we instead let people 'vote' with those dollars and
pounds down at the supermarket any day of the week.
And the remarkable thing about doing it that way is that
not only do those wanting cornflakes and Weetabix get
what they want, almost everybody does, too.

The market enables people to express their decisions directly and far better than any elected legislature has ever been able to do.

'Choosing breakfast cereal is a matter of personal choice,' you snort. 'The things that government provides have to be provided for everyone together.'

Really? Clearly some of what government spends must be spent by the state centrally, if it is to be spent at all. The portion spent on providing an opening ceremony for the Olympic Games or for defence, for example. But what about the rest?

Think of a traditional classroom. Rows of seats facing one blackboard. In front of which would have stood one teacher. Often there would have been one primary and one secondary school in the neighbourhood. One size had to fit pretty much everyone.

Or think of health care. The great mid-twentieth-century medical advances were made in treating common ailments: TB, polio, typhus, measles. Populations got a lot healthier once the common treatment to these ailments could be rolled out universally to everyone.

Or ponder pensions. Most people for much of the past century had remarkably similar work patterns. They usually entered the labour market at the same stage, perhaps even doing the standard number of years of military service first. They worked the requisite number of years, before retiring at the set age.

But look at how the world is changing.

Instead of one blackboard in one classroom, children tend to work in groups, with a more tailor-made approach. Tests and exams are less a measure of where the child is performing in relation to the rest of the class, and more a way of assessing what they know as individuals. Children tend to specialise and choose between subjects earlier and earlier.

Consider the big advances in medical science today. They tend to be the treatments that involve more tailor-made treatments, rather than the blockbuster breakthroughs of yesteryear. New treatments are increasingly niche, improving clinical outcomes for a smaller range of patients. There have even been some drugs developed for use by one, single individual patient.

Instead of uniform work patterns, more and more people have what you might call 'portfolio' careers. Not only do they change jobs, but they might not necessarily spend much of their time in a formal employer–employee relationship, instead working on specific projects. For millions of people, pension provision and retirement ages are no longer decided by the state. They are things that they must plan for themselves.

We have a one-size-fits-all approach to public services, with national curriculums, national health plans and national retirement ages, partly because that was the only way many public services could be provided in the past. But increasingly public services can become a matter of personal choice and preference.

So why not let people 'vote' directly as citizen-consumers on how they get some of those services, rather than keep pretending that their one in several million votes at election time makes any difference?

WHAT iGOVERNMENT MIGHT LOOK LIKE

According to news reports in early 2012, British Prime

Minister David Cameron has had a tailor-made app built for his iPad. 'Dave's dashboard' enables the PM to 'see real-time data on government performance, polling, the markets, inflation statistics'[101] and much else besides. Gosh.

Those who spun this story no doubt did so hoping that it would show how modern and thoroughly dot com the government is. 'Look,' they seemed to be saying, 'with all that information at his finger tips, Digital Dave can run things better!'

Modern? The idea behind Digital Dave's dashboard is more retro than a ZX Spectrum.

There is nothing modern about making public administration more inwardly accountable to one man sitting at the heart of government, whatever sort of computer he happens to have. What would be modern would be to make public administration outwardly accountable to the rest of us.

As Hayek told us, there has been no shortage of attempts to bring together information in one spot to enable politicians to try to decide things for the rest of us. Government has long been in the business of gathering masses of data in one spot in Whitehall, on an iPad or otherwise.

The Prime Minister's new iPad app, several pet pundits breathlessly informed us, would enable him to 'judge the success or failure of ministers with reference to performance-related data'. How quaint. What would be really transformative would be to enable each of us – not just the Prime Minister – to judge the success or failure of public services, by putting information on to our iPads and putting choice in front of us each individually.

Forget about what data Digital Dave gets on his iPad, what will matter is what data such technology puts on everyone else's.

Forget about how the British Prime Minister might be able to use the new technology to keep track of his own government. It is going to make the machinery of the state responsive to the rest of us.

As the President of Estonia recently put it, 'e-government has nothing to do with people in government having computers'.[102] Or what kind of apps they have on their computers, he might have added.

Already, digital technology is starting to allow us to choose for ourselves things that until recently Dave and Co. decided for us.

Like many parents, I recently discovered that my iPad or laptop can double up as a TV channel for my two-year-old. Instead of leaving it to CBeebies or Nickelodeon, dad becomes programmer-in-chief. In our household, that usually means endless *Peppa Pig* and *Dora the Explorer*. Different children, different households, tailor-made TV viewing.

But what happens when our children step inside the classroom?

They walk into a 1990-something world where there just isn't that level of personalisation and choice. Britain has a national curriculum that details what children must learn from the age of three. In the US, the federal government regulates not only what children are taught, but how. No Child Left Behind teaches like it's 1995.

Government officials commission education for our child, using our tax money – in Britain it is about £6,000 per child each year. They select the curriculum

content in much the same way that television producers decided what they thought was good for us. If you
are really lucky, you might have some kind of choice
between two or three schools, the way we used to have
a choice between a few TV channels.

This is all about to change. Just as digital technology
gave us an explosion of choice, to the point where we
are deciding what and when we view things, so too will it
enable us to personalise what each individual child learns.

Parents will be able to use their child's share of the
education budget to buy an education package that
suits not every child aged eight or twelve, but Tom or
Stephanie. You could purchase Tom and Stephanie's
education modules using your £6,000 of credits much
as you purchase anything else. Most of what you buy
could be from the same, single education provider
located at a single site. Others might prefer to buy a
range of learning from different providers.

Instead of a national curriculum, parents and teachers could tailor-make a personalised study plan for
your own child based on their individual needs, ability
and ambition.

Outrageous?

Here's a thought. Almost a fifth of children in London
have English as their second language. Think of what it
might mean to a whole classroom if a large chunk of the
kids need extra help. So why not enable those children
that need it to have a study plan that gives them the
extra help they need? A personalised study plan that
gave Pyotr extra English lessons would not interfere
with Peter's learning. Peter's need for additional maths
would not interfere with Pyotr's. Each day of Pyotr's
and Peter's learning would be designed to meet their

respective needs, not devised to fulfil some common denominator curriculum.

British ministers recently suggested that every nine-year-old in the country ought to know their maths times tables. Bravo, you might think. But think it through.

If Pyotr is ready to learn his maths tables aged eight, why shouldn't he? But if Peter is not ready to learn his until he is eleven or twelve, to whom does it matter? It only really matters to Peter – and if he is not ready until he is eleven, he is not ready. Why should it be any business of a politician in Whitehall?

The education system ought to adapt to fit the needs of the child, rather than try to fit a child around the needs of the education system.

'But if every child did their own thing, there would be chaos!' you interject. 'We need every child to study the same things to give them something in common. Standardised teaching gives us social cohesion.'

We've had thirty years of highly prescriptive, top-down curriculum-based teaching in Britain. It has failed to provide common cultural reference points or social cohesion. Judging by the summer 2011 riots, some might say it has achieved the opposite.

It is not central direction from government – in the classroom or anywhere else – that gives us our common cultural reference points. H. E. Marshall's classic English history text book – *Our Island Story* – was published in 1905, long before there was any kind of national curriculum. It provided a common narrative of England's past to generations of schoolchildren, without ever appearing on any government-approved teaching list.

Social cohesion happens organically. It occurs

when people find that – no matter how different their background or circumstances – they came by their own path to hold the same things in common. It happens when almost every household with three-year-old girls discovers that they somehow all watch the same episodes of *Peppa Pig* and *Dora the Explorer*.

Software already allows teachers to track class progress each year. Why not have software packages that enable mum and dad to track their child's progress? Instead of an end of year report, it could be a score-card, available online, in real time.

Far from encouraging solitary learning, apps and software would open up new possibilities for working collaboratively in groups. Perhaps even with children in other classrooms, schools and countries altogether.

Self-selection in the age of apps need not stop with schooling.

Every child could get a personalised learning account. Every person could have their own personalised health account – just like they already do in Singapore. Who knows, as well as government paying money into it, perhaps we might be allowed to contribute ourselves, possibly in lieu of paying taxes.

Over the past decade, governments in Britain, the United States and Europe have spent billions attempting to construct electronic medical records. Many of the costly IT schemes have consumed enormous amounts of taxpayer money.

But do we really need these 'mainframe'-type data systems? Back in the late 1970s, many thought that big, central hyper-expensive mainframe computers were the way to provide the computer architecture of the future. Today we know that computing power is networked, millions of desktops and laptops linked to each other and to servers. Perhaps medical records will go the same way. Instead of big, costly IT systems, our medical records will be managed by us. Perhaps using apps, costing a few pounds.

Personalised health accounts. Personalised medical records and clinical choices. A public health system that is focused on the public – every single one of them.

Almost any public service that is currently provided to individuals or families could be tailormade in this way. Social care budgets could be entirely personalised, so that families could ensure their loved ones get the care that suits their needs. Retirement would no longer be set at an arbitrary date. Why not allow each individual to have their own public pension retirement plan the way people in the private sector take for granted?

Nor need hyper-personalisation stop with public services we receive as individuals. Local community groups could download the decision-making process that decides how they spend public money. A local library could be managed by those who use it, with spending decisions made locally rather than by remote officials.

Radical? Hardly. Governments have been moving this way in many Western states for a decade or more. Increasingly governments are no longer just monopoly providers of key public services. Indeed, they are not even always monopoly commissioners either. Glacial though the pace of change might be, governments increasingly allow end users to self-commission their own public services.

What is new is not merely that digital technology

makes greater personalisation technically possible. It demolishes many of the obstacles that have been holding back these changes.

'BUT YOU CAN'T TRUST THE PEOPLE!'

Back in 1937, über-technocrat Douglas Jay declared that Britain's 'housewives as a whole cannot be trusted'. It would be unwise, he insisted, to leave it to such people 'to buy all the right things where nutrition and health are concerned. This is really no more than an extension of the principle according to which the housewife would not trust a child of four to select the week's purchases.'[103]

Even today, there are those who presume that only college-educated, preppy middle-class parents can raise healthy, happy families.

The rest of us, I hope, recognise that most adults have their own children's best interests at heart. Most mums and dads want what is best for their children. That is not to say that everyone makes rational choices all the time. And nor, tragically, are all parents good parents – even if biological parents are better custodians of children than any government agency yet created. But unless like Mr Jay you regard most people as no more reliable than a four-year-old child, you will accept that most people, most of the time, can be trusted to pursue their own interests.

'That might be so,' you insist, 'but how could you possibly trust a parent that never got school grade maths and English to make decisions for their child's education?'

Okay. So your case against letting people decide things for themselves – just like Douglas Jay's – boils down to the assumption that some folk just aren't smart enough to know what is right.

But is that not the point?

Almost none of us on our own could ever be clever enough to know what is right for our kids. Even the brightest physicist mum or polymath dad would have difficulty devising an entire curriculum for their child in isolation. Could anyone honestly say that they know all that their children need to know?

All of us need collective wisdom to know what our children need to learn. The question is: how do we assemble that collective knowledge?

Today we try to assemble all that collective wisdom the wrong way. We seek to do it by design, putting together a band of experts. We leave it to a few public officials and expert educationalists to immerse themselves in the facts and draw up a national curriculum for everyone.

No matter how many facts they take into account, no matter how wise they are, no matter how flexible they try to make their grand scheme, collective intelligence assembled by design is never very clever.

Collective intelligence by top-down design – call it Jay's way for short – does not work. As Hayek understood, no matter how expert Mr Jay, it is impossible to assemble perfect knowledge that way.

Even if you were to hand Mr Jay David Cameron's super duper new iPad, with its all-knowing Prime Ministerial app, you would never have perfect knowledge so as to allow either Mr Jay or Mr Cameron to do things by top-down design for the rest of us.

How many of the Mr Jays who designed national curriculums in the West a quarter of a century ago understood that every child should be taught to touch-type as a matter of routine? Before the advent of the PC, typing was seen as a skill for women wanting to be secretaries to acquire after leaving school. Today we recognise it is a basic skill everyone needs to get by.

Or consider the school timetable. For years we have left it to the Mr Jays to decide not only what schools teach, but when their terms start and school holidays begin. Thanks to doing things Jay's way, most British schools close their gates for six or seven weeks each summer. Why?

Because back in eighteen hundred and something a great many Britons lived in rural communities, and the kids were needed to help get the harvest in. To this day, schools in Scotland go back a couple of weeks later than in most of the rest of Britain. Why? Scotland's cooler climate generally meant that the harvest was collected that much later on.

Might it not be time to organise school schedules on the basis of what suits children and families today? Shorter terms? More frequent holidays?

By leaving it to the 'experts' to design the school timetable, we don't even get to see these questions asked. Instead, we stick with a school timetable designed to meet the needs of the nineteenth-century agrarian calendar. So much for doing things Jay's way. Forget about Digital Dave's Prime Ministerial app, too. Digital technology allows us to do without either.

What if we could organise things differently to the way they have been run before? What if collective intelligence could be assembled without central, top-down design? What if we could harness collective wisdom not through an assembly of experts in government, but by an assembly of experts throughout the world?

Digital technology means that instead of a maths class for all of Year 6, it will soon be possible to have maths lessons designed for Amy. And another one for Beth.

Much more important than merely being technically feasible, the digital revolution will ensure that even if Amy's and Beth's parents have never studied maths, they will be able to recognise good maths teaching when they see it.

This might seem totally counter-intuitive. How can someone who has not studied maths know good maths teaching when they see it?

OUR COLLECTIVE BRAIN

Keep thinking about iPads. Not necessarily the Prime Minister's one, but any old iPad. Think of all those tightly packed microchips inside its slender space. Contemplate its printed circuits and liquid crystal screen. Ponder the software codes – or apps – downloaded on it.

As you think of it, perhaps you assume that somewhere in California or China there sits a technological genius who built it all. Is there a Mr Ipad? Or Ms Ipad PhD? Or you think of the late Steve Jobs, perhaps?

Here's a thought: no one person on the planet knows how to produce that iPad from scratch. No one ever has, and most likely no one ever will.

The original team of engineers at Apple might have put together a highly detailed and complex blueprint, but they did so with chips that others had built and created. They coopted someone else's LED technology for the screen. The designers utilised someone else's plastic coating for the cover. And however much the engineers might have immersed themselves in the construction of the hardware, the software on the iPad is the product of many more design teams scattered across the planet.

No matter how detailed and brilliant the engineers' original design for that iPad, and no matter how innovative an idea, it is not the exclusive product of any one person's intelligence. Nor does knowledge of all the processes that went into creating it sit within one individual's head. It is the product of a vast, sprawling network of human intelligence.

Indeed, I would argue that the true genius of your iPad is not merely that it is built by collective intelligence. It is built in order to be programmed by collective intelligence, with apps designed all over the planet by thousands of people.

We use this collective brain – brought to us via specialisation and exchange – to assemble not only iPads but even the most ordinary and mundane household objects around us.[104] The collective brain not only produces all these material objects around us, but it enables dunderheads like me to obtain them.

Imagine if you walked into a mobile phone shop and the manager had removed all the prices and covered up the brands. If you could see neither the prices nor the brands, you would be shopping in isolation, left to make judgements about the relative worth or value based on ... probably guesswork.

Prices do not just tell you what the shopkeeper is willing to sell you something for. They also signal every other customer's assessment of the product's worth.

Prices are decided collectively – they are the aggregate judgement of thousands, perhaps millions, of people.

It is this collective market intelligence that enables someone like me to purchase a sophisticated electronic gizmo at a reasonable price. It allows me to know what good looks like. Everyone else's decision is helping me make mine.

This does not only allow me to buy the right kind of phone to suit me, without paying far over the odds. It allows people who know nothing about the workings of the internal combustion engine to try to accurately gauge the worth of a secondhand car. It allows us to feed our families in supermarkets without knowing much about nutrition.

In precisely the same way, the wisdom of the market would help parents who might not be themselves educated to make judgements about what kind of education to commission for their kids.

'It's all very well using prices and brands to help shoppers choose the shopping. But surely you couldn't use prices and brands to select your child's education?'

Perhaps the idea of an Oxford University-approved science curriculum or a Stanford-backed maths programme makes you scoff?

Until, of course, you realise that an Oxford University-approved science curriculum and a Stanford maths programme are precisely what attract tens of thousands of young people to want to study at both Oxford and Stanford. And makes thousands choose to sit university exam board examinations.

But even so, perhaps before you commit your child to studying a particular programme, you want some assurance about what it is that they might be learning.

The market signals of price and brand alone might not be enough to satisfy you.

But this is why the internet will be so transformative. It will additionally allow us to have so much more than market-derived intelligence as to what constitutes good.

OUR COLLECTIVE BRAIN IS ABOUT TO GET BIGGER

The digital revolution is not just another technological leap forward, like the invention of the wheel or the sail. It will bring in its wake even more profound changes than merely the expansion of our productive capabilities.

Trade and exchange are what makes us human. They distinguish us from all other creatures, and are what gives us our collective brain.

The digital revolution will not simply allow us to trade more widely – as the wheel or the sail once did. The digital revolution will enable us to trade and exchange and specialise in a completely different way, too. Instead of only contractual exchange, we are about to discover that we can build vast webs of collective intelligence on the basis of reciprocal exchange, too.

Contractual exchange meant a Stone Age hand axe for a cowrie shell, perhaps. Or a barrel of oil for $100 today, maybe. However complex the web of exchange, it is all about trading something for something.

But what if the internet allowed not merely contractual exchange, but a different sort of exchange entirely?

We all know how the internet has enhanced our ability to buy and sell things – more contractual exchange. eBay, Amazon, Gumtree – these websites allow millions of individuals to trade with millions of others. They allow extraordinarily niche, specialised markets. They enable the supply of things – from secondhand books to Star Wars memorabilia – to match demand.

But ask yourself this: do you spend more time online engaged in contractual exchanges on buyer/seller sites like eBay or Amazon, or engaged in all that other stuff you do online?

I spend vastly more of my time doing the 'other stuff'. Facebook updates here. Tweets on Twitter. Photo sharing. Reading other people's blogs and posting my own.

None of that is contractual exchange. We don't tend to do it for the money. You don't – I hope – count the number of tweets you expect to get back before you send a tweet. It would be odd if you posted photos on Facebook and complained that your friends short-changed you with too few of their holiday snaps in return.

But it is still a form of exchange – perhaps you might call it reciprocal exchange. Yet it is as real as any other kind of exchange.

When you stop to think about it, an awful lot of the internet is non-contractual, reciprocal exchange of one kind or another.

The internet did not invent reciprocal exchange. You see it when someone in your apartment block helps your elderly neighbour carry her heavy shopping. Or when you do things that are neighbourly.

Yet this kind of non-contractual, reciprocal exchange only really seems to happen in small, niche communities. While you might pick up litter in your village or street, you would be unlikely to wander around London doing the same.

Reciprocal exchange might be commonplace in niche communities, but because niche communities are precisely that – small and specific – there tends not to be a great deal of reciprocal exchange. Until now.

The internet is an almost endless, sprawling network of niche communities. Niche becomes norm. Quite suddenly, the kind of reciprocal exchange that only took place in the margins offline becomes ubiquitous online. Non-contractual exchange becomes almost routine, rather than exceptional.

Contractual exchange and specialisation have enabled humans to coordinate the actions of millions in a way that works. It has produced not just hand axes, pizzas and mobile phones. It has lifted *Homo sapiens* from the swamp to the stars.

But imagine where humans might go if we could begin to coordinate the energies and efforts of millions through an organic network not just of contractual exchange, but of reciprocal exchange.

Wikipedia is just one example of online collectivism. There are hundreds of different wiki platforms. Digg allows articles to be shared. Shapeways enables 3D designers to share their designs.

Each of these online communities is niche. No matter how much the web traffic passing through these sites makes them the crowded online equivalent of Piccadilly Circus or Times Square, in terms of building and maintaining the sites, they remain small, village-like communities. Wikipedia might be read by millions, but it is in the main written and edited by a few thousand. Millions of people might be on Twitter at any one time, but they are each looking at a very niche stream of tweets.

Non-contractual internet exchange is sometimes looked upon as a form of 'dot communism', a kind of online socialism. I find this description odd. It is the free market that is a decentralised, free-forming, collective network of exchange, sometimes involving millions, perhaps billions of people. It is the free market that is best understood as a sprawling network of specialisation and exchange. Just because people are making those exchanges on a reciprocal, rather than a contractual, basis does not make it any less of a market. If anything, this market in advice, designs, ideas, opinions, photos and pretty much everything else people post for nothing online is even more of a free market than the free market produced by contractual trade.

Market intelligence – information about price and brand – helps people who know nothing about the products and services they are seeking to buy make astute judgements about value. Non-market intelligence produces an even greater plethora of signals to guide us.

When we book holidays online, or buy toys on Amazon, we no longer have just the sellers' word to go by. We can see what other products people like us bought. We can read independent reviews written by people like us. They did not write those online reviews because they were paid to. It is again another kind of reciprocal exchange – collective intelligence given to us by the crowd.

Our collective brain doesn't only allow us to buy consumer items. It will also enable a parent who has had little formal education to recognise what a good education for their child looks like.

Online parental peer review is already enabling some

of the most disadvantaged mums and dads in Britain to make highly complex judgements about the needs of their children – and ensure those needs are then met.

When I first became an MP, a steady stream of parents of children with special needs contacted me wanting my help. Officialdom had failed to give their kids the kind of education they believed their children needed – and they needed my help to hack through the jungle of bureaucracy that was put in their way to stop them. In a little over three years, I helped take over thirty cases to tribunal – and the parents won almost every time.

Then suddenly the flow of parents dried up. Within the space of a few months I suddenly found they just weren't contacting me for help any more. I was puzzled.

Was it because there were suddenly no more parents dissatisfied with the education their kids were getting? Sadly, no. Data showed that the number of children with special needs kept rising and the number of cases taken to tribunal was depressingly high. Perhaps the education authorities wised up and started being more accommodating? If only. Maybe it was me, and something to do with the way I was working? Nope. I continued to advertise my availability and willingness to help as before.

The big change was the internet. Round about the time that almost everyone started to have email, parents began to share the know-how needed to fight and win cases without having to come to me. They even replicated the Word document files containing the necessary legal text with each other, so no need to get it from the local MP.

The change just sort of happened, without any kind of central direction. All of a sudden, informal, reciprocal collaboration meant parents of children with some extraordinarily complex needs were able to identify those needs – and ensure they were met with remarkable success.

Imagine if we had an education system that harnessed, rather than tried to exclude, this kind of spontaneous parental peer review. It is no longer a case of imagining it. It is starting to happen.

A few years ago, a dozen or so families in Clacton decided that they were going to boycott a local school. They had compared what their children were learning with what children in other schools were learning, and flatly refused to send their children to what they regarded as a substandard school. Reluctantly, they looked to home-educate their children, clubbing together at their own expense, instead.

As they did so, they were forced to ask questions about what their children ought to learn. Linking up via the internet with other parent groups around the country, they decided that they would not slavishly follow the national curriculum. Instead they decided that they – together with those professional teachers they hired to teach their children – could devise a programme of learning that drew on the experience of others.

How did this experiment in collaboratively designing a learning programme work out? The children's SAT scores and GCSE results turned out to be consistently above average.

Taken aback by the number of families involved, the local education experts were eventually embarrassed into giving this group of Essex mums and dads an ad hoc home education grant worth several thousand pounds a year. This home education grant might have only amounted to a fraction of the £6,000-and-something per child pot of money that the education authority had available, but giving the grant established an important precedent.

It was not merely recognition of the fact that parents were able to commission education for their children. It was acknowledgement of the fact that parents can know what good looks like. And can do a better job of commissioning education than the education authorities.

At the same time, parents of special needs children in Essex, some of whom have zero expertise, are starting to collaborate 'outside the system' to identify, for example, the kind of speech therapy their child needs. Instead of waiting for the local education special needs coordinator to fill in all the forms – and then explain that there is a waiting list for speech therapists – they are locating speech therapists directly. They are able to because email and the internet allow them to pool together a level of knowledge that previously only the experts would have had access to.

Armed with the kind of knowledge that once only experts had, they are able to overcome official intransigence that says they – and their children – must stand in line and leave it to the experts to decide what is best of their families.

There is now even a government Bill before Parliament – the Children and Families Bill – that will enshrine into law the principle that parents are able to commission educational services for their children, giving mums and dads of children with special needs personalised budgets.

Imagine if mums and dads were free to commission

for their child the speech therapy package that was
desperately needed all along.

Allowing every parent to commission their child's
education would not leave them isolated in a world
of anarchy and chaos. The digital future will not be a
world of atomised individualism. On the contrary, as
those Clacton parents discovered, it will be a world of
dramatically expanded collectivism – but collectivism
without the state.

'But what if parents still get it wrong?' you persist.

Some people will always make wrong choices.
However much collective intelligence you assemble to
help folk make the right choices, sometimes they won't.
Allowing all those British housewives to 'select the
week's purchases', the way Douglas Jay found so objec-
tionable, means that from time to time mistakes will be
made. Some folk will buy chilli powder, mistaking it for
food colouring, with disastrous culinary consequences.
More seriously, some people end up obese.

In the same way, if you allow parents to buy the
wrong kind of course for their child, some will do so.

But it is trying to do things Mr Jay's way that does far
more to prevent children with special needs – or any
other kind of needs – getting the education that they
need today. Most children needing speech therapy in
Essex have to wait for it. After years slip by, some never
get it at all. Doing things Mr Jay's way means standing
in line, the way we used to have to queue for food when
Douglas Jay and Co. rationed that, too.

Giving parents consumer power, and the power to
harness peer review, means that even those without
school grade maths will be able to know a good education when they see one.

'Jo is doing the Letter Land course? Jimmy's teachers recommended that he learn the alphabet that way too.' So you add it to the software that schedules Jimmy's learning plan.

'Those reviews say that that maths module is difficult. But it'll help Amy if she wants to study chemistry or physics next year.' So Amy has an education plan tailormade to her ambition to become a doctor by people who have never studied medicine.

RULE BY THE CITIZEN-CONSUMER

'This might be possible in theory,' you say, 'but it is never going to happen.'

Why not? Perhaps you think that the voter won't like it? Think again.

Politically, it is not as though Western voters tend to have much confidence in the remote elites who preside over them. What makes you so confident that they won't reject the overpriced system of government those elites have foisted on them? It's not like it's delivered value for money. It has left us broke.

Already the past decade has seen a decisive shift in Western social values.

After decades of believing that it should be up to the state to provide such things for us, a clear majority of British people now support the idea that those able to afford to do so should be able to buy better health care and education.[105]

There has been a decisive fall in the number of people who support higher taxes to pay for public services. In 2002, 63 per cent of people believed that taxes should rise to pay for more state-provided services. Today that number has fallen by more than half.[106] People increasingly respect the right of individuals to spend their own money on health and education, but are reluctant to leave it to officialdom to do it for them.

Libertarian ideals are going mainstream, mid-twentieth-century faith in Fabianism fading.

Redistribution is out. For a generation or more, British voters have tended to believe that government should redistribute wealth. Those days are over, with a clear long-term trend away from support for a redistributive state.[107] In 1991, almost 60 per cent supported spending more on benefits. By 2009, that number had fallen to almost one in four.

A growing majority of voters now regard poverty not as a product of social injustice, requiring state intervention, but as a consequence of personal lifestyle preferences and choices. There is a growing tendency to blame individuals – not wider society – for personal outcomes.

Nor is this a distinctively British phenomenon. Social attitudes amongst the i-generation are shifting towards greater personal autonomy, and away from top-down statism throughout the West. In every country, those who have grown up free to select for themselves playlists and iPod content seem less willing to leave it to officialdom to select for them the vital things in life.

Perhaps most significant of all, the latest survey of British Social Attitudes found that 'older respondents are more likely to take a collectivist and less consumerist stance'. Not only are attitudes shifting, but it is a generational shift.

A politically disengaged electorate recognises that as long as it only has the power to elect representatives, it has little power at all. Power to decide things for ourselves comes not only from the power to elect an assembly of representatives to rule over us, but from the power to participate in spontaneous exchange.

It took a decade or so to happen, but thanks to the internet no one needs to pay more than the lowest price in the world for books, toys, consumer goods and a whole lot of other things that you can find on Amazon and elsewhere. Before Amazon, your local electrical store might have added on a local premium price. But unless you were willing to shop around, you had to make do.

Not any more. Now the lowest price becomes the price for everyone.

The internet will do the same to public goods too, driving down prices. Governments currently charge us for services that the market is able to supply at a far lower price. Increasingly, people can see this.

The internet allows information about public spending to be broken down into what it costs to provide the things that we as individuals consume. Instead of being a debate about unimaginable millions or billions, public spending starts to be about individual payments. And once the debate about public spending comes down from the macroeconomic stratosphere, and starts to be about what the treatment we get costs, it suddenly becomes clear that public services funded out of taxation don't look quite so 'free' at all.

We all like the idea of getting something for free. Something-for-nothing sounds great. But from promotional chocolate bars handed out in the high street to state education in the classroom for the kids, what do you notice about all those things that we are supposedly given for free? You have to take what you are given.

That is not really a problem when you are being unexpectedly offered a new chocolate bar. You don't like it? Simple. Bin it.

But what happens when the 'free' service you are being offered is your child's education, but it is not quite to your – or their – tastes?

In fact, unlike promotional chocolate bars, public services turn out to be anything but free. We have paid for them via taxation, sometimes many times over. Public services in many Western states are only 'free' in the sense that you have to take what you are given.

Because you are not paying the person directly supplying you with the service, you have no consumer power. Try suggesting to the teachers in a British state school that your child ought to learn Spanish, not French. It would be as pointless as demanding the person handing out free promotional chocolate bars gives you your favourite bagel instead. It's not on offer.

Walk into a restaurant and order something from the menu, but request some minor alternation – no onion in the side salad, or extra cheese topping. The chances are that the staff will do what they can to meet your needs.

Try asking for some minor alternation to what is on the menu from Britain's monolithic public services. You will most likely get a blank stare.

As a paying customer, you have power. But if we are not allowed to pay for things, we have to make do with what we are given.

In Britain and much of western Europe, 'free' health and education turn out to mean that you must take what you are given. Indeed, often the system expressly forbids you from paying lest – horror of horrors – the service users start to demand the things they want.

In Britain, officials decide the size of the health budget because health care is a state monopoly. Even if a private individual wanted to increase their own personal part of the health budget by £100 to get something better, they cannot. The national health budget is kept down even if individuals freely and willingly want it to go up.

This explains why in Britain the NHS is persistently underfunded by all governments. Regardless of which party is in office, government more or less constantly fails to provide it with enough cash compared to what people would be prepared to spend on those same services – if they could access them without the delays.

Citizen-consumers are not going to be prepared to meekly take what they are given.

On June 14 2012, a nine-year-old Scottish schoolgirl, Martha Payne, was sitting in her classroom when she was ordered out by teachers.

Her crime? She had been taking photographs of her school food, and posting the pictures onto her website, NeverSeconds.blogspot.co.uk.

So unsavoury did the food she and her classmates were expected to eat appear, the web postings provoked local controversy. Stories began to appear in the local *Dunoon Observer*.

Embarrassed by what people were able to see online, local officials from Argyll and Bute council did what officials like to do in such situations. They issued a decree banning children from taking photos of their food in all school dining facilities.

That particular piece of idiocy merely provoked an

even greater controversy. Instead of being just a local news item, stories about heavy-handed officials attempting to bully Martha started to appear in the national press. The story started to run on the BBC news.

Eventually, live on BBC Radio 4's flagship lunchtime news programme, the head of Argyll and Bute council, Roddy McCuish, had to back down.

What was striking is not just that the local authority's insistence that Martha should not be able to post photos of her food online proved untenable. So, too, was the insistence by council officials that the food on Martha's plate was 'fully compliant with agreed national nutritional standards'.

Who said it complied? And complied with what?

What did it matter what the national standards might say? Everyone could see that what landed on Martha's plate looked revolting. Martha's lunch might well have complied with officialdom's idea of good food. It did not comply with what most folk would regard as good food.

Suddenly the internet not only makes accountability outward to the individual user. It makes the whole paraphernalia for top-down decision making, through which you elect councillors and politicians to agree national standards in the first place, look quaint and ridiculous.

The average health authority in England and Wales spends enough money each year to pay for comprehensive medical insurance cover on the open market for every local family. What makes you think that people won't want to take their slice of the money and do just that? Eventually they will get fed up with waiting in line and start to demand that they do.

Of course the elite won't like it.

But iPolitics means that it won't really matter what the elite want. It is what voters demand that will count. If thousands of mums and dads start to demand that they – not the latest in a long line of politicians – control their child's £6,000 education budget because the elite are so hopeless at spending it, they have the power to make that happen.

The power of the masses will be augmented by the power of maths.

No matter what politicians' laws proclaim, the laws of mathematics usually prevail. And the laws of maths say that when the state is spending 20, 30 or even 40 per cent more than it is taking in tax, you have to lose a similar-size chunk of government eventually.

You think that politicians will prevent that from happening? Do you think that they managed to stop it from happening in Greece? Do you suppose anyone in Athens was elected to shut down their big, bloated, cradle-to-grave welfarism? On the contrary, politicians promised to prevent it. People took to the streets to stop it.

But it went ahead and happened all the same. Large chunks of the Greek welfare system have simply gone.

That's what happens when the money runs out and you cannot keep hiding the costs; you don't just have government cuts. You have to cut government.

The digital revolution means that Western states will no longer be able to tax the few to fund the illusions of the many. Technological change means that income tax, through which a tiny minority pick up the bill for Big Government, will gradually give way to flatter taxes on consumption and property.

And once every household faces a similar-size bill for all that extra government, the question of whether we still need it all will sit centre stage. It will no longer be part of the political agenda in Western elections. It will be the election agenda.

As in the nineteenth century, how much – or how little – officials should tax people will become the defining issue in politics.

'Shrinking the size of the state is remarkably difficult,' the free-market-when-they-want-your-vote politicians tell us. 'It can't be done.'

Of course it can't be done if you rely on the kind of elite officialdom who made government so big in the first place to make it happen. But it can and will be done by the maths and the masses, and by technology.

Government in Britain, America and Europe has something like $20,000 to spend per person each year on various services. If government finds that it only has $19,000 to spend, or even $15,000, it might have no choice other than to allow us to self-commission as much of that budget as we can for ourselves.

As every business owner knows, when the person making the purchase is not the same person paying for it, costs go up. When it is government buying services on our account, but with our money, we almost inevitably get poor value. Somehow when officialdom is buying the goods and the services for us there seem to be overhead costs somewhere. When the money runs out, getting citizens to self-commission services for themselves will suddenly start to look like the least painful way of eliminating some of those overheads.

Government won't need to put in place complex new

arrangements. Officialdom won't have to make plans for it, any more than Apple tries to arrange that someone builds all those apps that make its iPad come alive. A legal right for citizens to take their share of the money and opt out is all it needs.

Maths and the self-interest of millions will do the rest.

Perhaps the only other thing our politicians need also to do is to learn to do nothing.

In Belgium for four years this is precisely what happened. In 2007, following a fractious and indecisive election, the various political parties refused to work together to form a coalition government. So until 2011, Belgium went without one.

As the Flemish Democrats bickered with the Wallonian Something-or-Other, new laws went unmade. Fresh regulations were not drafted. Initiatives untaken. Officialdom simply stopped doing things.

And then something remarkable started to happen.

Because so much of what officialdom does decays over time of its own accord, many of the existing regulations and red tape simply became redundant. Businesses got used to the rules, and learnt to work round them.

That regulatory drag caused by officials doing things started to grow weaker. The Belgian economy started to grow stronger.

Bizarrely, given the economic storm brewing all around her, Belgium started to prosper. Her GDP grew faster than expected in every quarter for four years. So much so that Belgium today now exports more to India than Britain.

Described as a 'crisis' by members of the political class, Belgium's four years without a government was anything but. Indeed, Belgium's no-government proved to be one of the most successful administrations in modern Belgian history.

While Greek politicians were debating something called a 'New Deal for Greek Youth', Spanish politicians ran up ever larger debts and Italian politicians lurched from one scandal to another. Belgian politicians? They did nothing. Which country is in better shape today?

If the purpose of government is to enable citizens to grow more prosperous and free, the Belgian administration of 2007 to 2011 shows how it can be done: stop government from doing things. Once folk are free to opt out, government needs do surprisingly little for the iState to become reality.

Would downsizing the state provoke social disorder? Watching smoke drifting across south London during the riots last summer, it seems to me that Big Government is pretty good at producing social disorder all by itself.

The elite, in whose interest government grew so big in the first place, will issue dark warnings. Cutting back on all those £100,000 education outreach coordinators, imply the education outreach coordinators, will mean anarchy and mayhem. Mobs of angry youths will rampage across a desolate urban landscape in search of extra maths tuition...

Oh please! Cutting the education and welfare budgets in Britain by half would hardly take us back to the slums of Victorian England. It would return us back to circa 2002.

With half those on the education payroll in Britain not actually teaching, it would be possible to halve the education budget and maintain exactly the same standard of teaching.

Everyone knows that if we sharply reduce the size of government there will be chaos and disorder. Everyone says so ... except they don't.

The 'everyone' telling us that we need Big Government turns out to be a remarkably small clique.

Draw back the curtain that shrouds the commentariat, and this 'everyone' turns out not to be some wise, omnipotent being. As Dorothy discovered in *The Wizard of Oz*, they turn out to be rather dull middle-aged men. Fakes. Secondhand dealers in ideas. No more qualified to decide how society might be organised than the humbug circus performer in Frank Baum's children's classic.

If public services were no longer provided by top-down design, but by the interactions of millions of members of the public who actually used them, you could do without all the coordinators. No planning, so no planners. No grand design, so no more designers. Shut down the department of business, innovation and skills. Let businesses innovate instead. Instead of a department for communities and local government, give control back to communities.

When your parents were your age, government was about a third smaller than it is today. When your grandparents were your age, it was about half the size.

Far from anarchy and disorder, there was an orderly progression in human affairs. Crime was lower. The economy generally grew faster. There was less long-term unemployment. There was faster technological innovation and more invention.

None of that is to say that life in the West was better back then than it is today. It wasn't – the world was less fair, less equal and less free. But that is the whole point. Life got better because government was smaller. Progress was possible. It will be again once we shrink the state.

CHAPTER 11

IS THE WEST STILL BEST?

The West is bust, but are we doomed?

Pick up a newspaper, or watch a current affairs programme, and there seems to be no shortage of pessimism about the West's prospects. But then one thing that the West has never lacked are those convinced of our imminent demise.

From scientists like Robert Malthus or Francis Galton, to historians such as Arnold Toynbee or Oswald Spengler, to philosophers like Friedrich Nietzsche or writers like HG Wells, a strong streak of doom has long pervaded Western thought. It might be that a sense of impending disaster is inevitable in a culture whose renaissance – or 'rebirth' – took place amidst the ruins of a Classical past. Or perhaps it is just because deep thinkers tend to be gloomy.

Whatever the reason, those predicting the West's imminent collapse over the past couple of hundred years have got it spectacularly wrong.

In the two centuries since Malthus predicted famine and pestilence, Europe's population has increased more than tenfold – and we are generally healthier and better fed than would have seemed imaginable back then.

In the hundred years since Spengler's *Decline of the West* warned us that technological advances would peter out, the West has enjoyed a century of the most extraordinary scientific achievement. Whatever Toynbee told us about history, he was not much good at telling us about the future. Far from retreating the way he warned, Western civilisation has expanded to encompass more people around the planet than ever.

HG Wells might have written about time travellers, but his work remains fiction, not forecast. And for all Nietzsche's bizarre ideas about supermen struggling for the future, superman remains – fortunately – a rather dated superhero.

But just because the doom-mongers have got it wrong, that does not mean that the demise of the West is not going to happen. The point about the boy who cried 'wolf, wolf' is that eventually there was a wolf.

Are the wolves at the West's door?

THE TWILIGHT OF THE WEST?

Forget the theorists and the philosophers for a moment. Consider some facts.

In 2000, the G6 group of the world's most advanced industrialised countries comprised the United States, Japan, Germany, France, Italy and Britain. In another decade or two, only America and Japan would make it on to any list of the top half-dozen world economies.

Already, the G6 has had to be turned into the G20. In order for Italy, France and Britain to make the guest list by 2030, it will have to be known as the G30. Or perhaps even the G50.

In 1973, the West's share of global GDP was almost

60 per cent. By 2003, it had fallen to 46 per cent – and by 2030,[108] it is forecast to be closer to 33 per cent. In other words, it will have halved within the space of two generations.

We are witnessing a massive pull of plant and capital away from the West towards the new economies of the East, as three centuries of Western economic hegemony come to an end. Asia is now the biggest market for many products, accounting for 35 per cent of all car sales and 43 per cent of mobile phones. Asia guzzles 35 per cent of the world's energy, up from 26 per cent in 1995. It has accounted for two-thirds of the increase in world energy demand since 2000.

In 2009, 40 per cent of global investment (at market exchange rates) took place in Asia, as much as in America and Europe combined. In finance, Asian firms launched eight of the ten biggest initial public offerings (IPOs) in 2009 and more than twice as much capital was raised through IPOs in China and Hong Kong last year as in America.[109]

In 1990, China's economy was about a third the size of the US economy. By 2015, some forecast that it will have overtaken the American economy. By 2030, it will be almost as large as the US, French, German and Italian economies combined, apparently.[110]

Does this really matter?

Back in 1820, Asia accounted for around 60 per cent of world wealth creation. So what if we are heading back to that kind of level again? Wealth creation is not, after all, a zero sum game. Just because Asia happens to hold 60 per cent of the pie again, it is a vastly bigger pie than before. Far from being our loss, Asia's ability to produce wealth is our gain, too.

End of Western economic hegemony

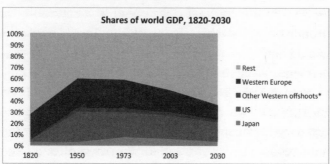

Source: *The West and the Rest in the World Economy*, Angus Maddison

If only it was just a question of the non-Western world catching up with the West, there would indeed be little to worry about. The trouble is that it is not just that the Rest are catching up – the West is slowing down.

Western countries are sinking under a massive burden of debt. Every American adult owes $180,000 of public debt. Every Japanese, $110,000. Every European, over $100,000.

In order for their economies to grow faster than their level of public debt has been increasing since 2007, the United States would need annual GDP growth of over 12.8 per cent, Japan 4.5 per cent and Europe 7.3 per cent.[111] Neither Europe nor the United States have ever enjoyed that level of sustained growth. Japan last expanded at that rate in the 1970s.

Western debt is growing faster than the West's economies could hope to expand. And Western debt is dragging down the West's capacity for future growth.

The West's long-term growth trend seems to be falling.

Since 1877, the United States economy has grown at

an average 3.5 per cent per year. Over the past decade or so, the US has fallen way behind that long-term trend. Indeed, in order to catch up, the US economy would need to expand by an unprecedented 5 per cent per annum for the next six or seven years.[112]

Between 1950 and 1973, western Europe grew an average of 4 per cent a year. Growth slowed down to about half that during the 1970s and 1980s. Since the mid-1990s, Europe's productivity growth has slowed sharply. Europe's long-term growth prospects appear less promising than at any time since the 1940s.

The West's rapid deindustrialisation, declared a generation of economists, was nothing to worry about. It was, they assured us, all part of a market-driven process of organic change. Factories and metal bashing in Europe and North America would give way to smooth-running service sector-driven economies. The mucky business of actually making things would move to Asia.

Except maybe today it doesn't look quite so simple.

What if Western deindustrialisation happened not because of any inexorable drive towards economic maturity, but because we put in place excessive regulation and taxation? Maybe large swathes of Detroit or Birmingham no longer produce any wealth not because of anything that has happened in Asia, but because of decisions made in the West that drove the wealth creation away?

As the West developed service-based economies, perhaps we deluded ourselves into thinking that that meant we could not at the same time continue to create wealth by making things, too. Shanghai and Mumbai can do banking and insurance, but I have yet to hear anyone from China or India explain that that means they have to give up manufacturing in order to do so.

Perhaps even more alarmingly, for all the digital innovation taking place around us, there is some evidence that the West is in certain ways actually becoming less innovative.

According to Tyler Cowen, author of *The Great Stagnation*, the era of peak innovation in America and the West has passed. It happened when government was a lot smaller. While raw GDP data show that the West continues to grow, Cowen suggests, the expanded role of government has distorted GDP figures upward, and economic expansion has been slowing down.

Others, such as Peter Thiel, the Silicon Valley guru, have suggested that despite the digital take off, the West is in reality experiencing a slowdown in the rate of technological progress.

Still others have pointed out how between 1996 and 1999, for example, the US Federal Drug Agency approved 157 new drugs. By 2006–09, the FDA approved almost half that amount. The length of time that it now takes to bring a drug to trial is now between seven and ten years.

Perhaps technological innovation is happening, but just not inside the West?

Why might the West have lost its spark? To see why, perhaps it is necessary to understand what made the West pre-eminent in the first place.

THE SECRET OF THE WEST'S SUCCESS

Imagine that an extra-terrestrial traveller zoomed by planet Earth in AD 1000. Perhaps, as they peered down at the blue planet, they might have shown a passing interest in those Earthlings far below.

Looking for the most advanced sign of intelligent

life, our wandering alien might focus first on the Chinese empire on the far eastern part of the Asian land mass. With large towns, canals, paper money, compass and gunpowder, our intergalactic friend might have expected China to have been the dominant player in human affairs over the coming millennium.

Casting around for the also-rans, our alien friend might have spotted some of the cities and temples produced by five thousand years of civilisation in India. Our fictional ET might also have looked approvingly at the mighty Abbasid Caliphate, or spotted Constantinople's Hagia Sophia, tucked away in the north eastern corner of the Byzantine Mediterranean.

Yet if our star traveller's gaze happened to wander across to the north western end of the Eurasian land mass – Europe – he would have spied only the occasional hovel amidst thick forests, with a few baronial castles here and there. There would have been almost nothing to suggest that it would be European civilisation that would do so much to shape human affairs for the next thousand years.

In AD 1000, Europeans weren't just poorer than Indians and Chinese. The per capita income of those living in Europe was below the global average.[113] Technologically, too, Europe lagged behind much of the rest of the planet.

So how come Europe ended up dominating much of the next millennium of human history? What was it that made Western civilisation pre-eminent?

Or to put it another way, why did the Chinese not circumnavigate the globe and discover Portugal? Or Indian adventurers initiate trade with Europe?

Was the rise of the West due to the Galileian or

Newtonian advances in science, perhaps? Was it because the West developed universities? If anything, China and the Islamic world were more scientifically advanced than Europe. Islam had distinguished seats of learning in Baghdad, Cairo and Fez.

Perhaps it was the printing press that gave the West take-off? The only trouble with that theory is that China invented printing – and not only didn't China take off, neither did printing in China.

Maybe it was advances in maritime technology? Again, China had the largest, most advanced fleet well into the second millennium.

The West's lead in terms of scientific discovery, learning, navigation and technology are all consequences of the West's ascendency, not causes of it.

The secret of the West's success lay elsewhere.

The West rose, suggests the Australian historian E. L. Jones in his book *The European Miracle*, because Europe, unlike the empires of the Ming, the Mughals or the Ottomans, was never a unified state. Power remained dispersed and diffused.

'But surely dispersed power would hinder, not help, a society to develop?' you might think. 'How could you direct development in a society where dispersed power made it impossible to coordinate things?'

That is precisely the point. It is the attempts to 'coordinate things' according to some kind of deliberate plan that hinders social and economic development. However counter-intuitive it might at first seem, Western society was remarkably innovative and dynamic because – until remarkably recently – power was so dispersed and constrained, little could be organised by deliberate design.

The West was, if you like, historically Hayekian. Or rather more Hayekian than the Rest.

It lacked the social and political institutions that might have enabled one person or elite to manage to run Europe uniformly according to any particular design – despite the best efforts of the medieval papacy, the Habsburgs, Napoleon and the Kaiser.

Whereas the empires of the East became centralised, heavily taxed and bureaucratised, Europe's statelets were in constant competition with one another. This allowed, to use modern jargon, 'systems competition'.

New ideas and approaches could be tried out in one state, and copied in others if seen to work. However arbitrarily a prince might exercise power in one domain, there was never a central authority capable of imposing restrictive practices across the whole of Europe.

Fragmented power prevented the rise of the kind of stifling, parasitical elites that hindered human progress for most of human history. It meant fewer of those disastrous grand designs loved by princes, priests, emperors and modern-day administrators.

Benign fragmentation allowed competition and innovation.

When King John II of Portugal rejected Christopher Columbus's hare-brained scheme to sail across the Atlantic in search of a new route to Asia, Columbus was able to appeal instead to Spain's Ferdinand and Isabella. One monarch's veto was not enough to hold back a great voyage of discovery.

When the Bourbon kings of France decided to expel their Protestant subjects, the Huguenots took their innovation and enterprise with them to England and beyond. The industry and ingenuity of one people were not lost to Europe as a whole by the actions of one despot.

It was not just people that could escape to a more benign part of Europe. Ideas and innovation could too.

When Copernicus and other scientific works were censored in France and Spain for challenging the doctrines of the Catholic Church, they were printed and passed on in Holland. Scientific ideas that were extinguished in one part of the continent were thus kept alive in another.

In the late Middle Ages and Early Modern period, it was amongst the independent city states of northern Italy and Flanders that many cultural and commercial innovations first appeared.

In competition with one another, city states asserted their independence from kings and emperors, claiming autonomous property rights. Merchants and guilds were able to obtain tax exemptions and the right to hold markets without having their trade expropriated by priests or princes.

Indeed, one particular city state with a maritime outlet – Venice – rose to become a great power, almost toppling Byzantium in 1204.

Europe not only had systems competition *between* different states, but increasingly *within* states, too.

However autocratic the Doge, Venice was a republic – one in which power was shared with the Great Council, or *Maggior Consiglio*. Power was never in the hands of a single hereditary king or family. If not democracy, it was oligarchy rather than monarchy.

So, too, within the seventeenth-century Dutch republic, where there was no single ruler, but a federation of states. Unlike the powerful centralised monarchies of France and Spain, in Holland, it was an assembly – the States-General – that jealously controlled the right to raise taxes.

And this model of dispersed power within a state produced something extraordinary.

Starting in the Dutch republic in the seventeenth century, for the first time in human history, GDP started to increase beyond any rise in the human population. In other words, GDP began to increase sharply in per capita terms.

This made the Dutch perhaps the first people to properly escape the Malthusian constraints and start to grow rich. Before the rise of the Dutch Republic, economic growth had, for most of human history, been extensive. That is to say it increased (or fell) in line with an overall rise (or fall) in the human population. It was in the seventeenth-century Dutch statelets, with dispersed and limited power, that humans first began to enjoy a per capita increase in living standards.

Despite having few natural resources, the Dutch dominated world trade in the seventeenth century, acquiring a vast overseas empire and a navy. Dutch merchants developed a system of banking and a stock exchange. Holland became, for a time, the wealthiest and most urbanised region on the planet.

Limited government – something that the Dutch republic acquired almost by accident – the English rebels of the 1640s fought for at Naseby. Putting to death a king who, like his peers in Spain and France, believed his right to reign was conferred from on high, in 1688 the English imported a Dutch king who brought with him a Dutch appreciation of the fact that the right to reign came from below.

And England, too, also began to escape the Malthusian trap, becoming perhaps only the second place on earth where GDP rose rapidly in per capita terms. She, also, started to trade with the world, acquiring a navy and the start of an overseas empire. Later still, England went one step further, not only discovering how to increase her per capita wealth, but discovering industrial production.

European states within which power was dispersed generally pulled ahead of those European states that remained centralised. Spain – whose feeble Cortes could not rein in the spending habits of an autocratic king – entered a downward economic spiral of debt and rising taxes. Absolutist France – a great power in the sixteenth century – had become an economic also-ran by the eighteenth.

However much centralisation induced stagnation and decline within any one individual European state, unlike the Oriental empires of the east, the follies of the French king or Habsburg emperors could not hold in check innovation across an entire civilisation. Always one or more parts of the mosaic that was the West were able to remain free from the kind of self-inflicted sclerosis that arrested development elsewhere.

And sure enough, between 1800 and 2006, the West's income per capita rose by an astonishing twenty-one times. In the rest of the world, it rose only eightfold.

How different things turned out to be in China.

Having been the most advanced civilisation on the planet in AD 1000, China spent much of the next millennium going backwards.

China did not just fall behind Europe over the following centuries. China by the end of the millennium had fallen behind China at the beginning of the millennium.

Someone living in China in 1950 would have been poorer than someone living in China a thousand years before. China's regression was not only relative, but in many regards absolute. Despite having invented printing, paper currency, the compass, gunpowder and much else, it was Europeans who had taken those inventions and applied them.

What went wrong?

Plague and invasions played a part. But what really held back China was China – or to be more precise, China's rulers.

While the West lacked centralised political authority, China was governed by a succession of imperial elites.

Power was centralised and innovation punished. Paperwork was imposed on traders, requiring them to keep onerous records – a 'regime of paperwork and harassment, endless paperwork and endless harassment'. A remote mandarinate, hostile to innovation and the unregulated, presided over the nooks and crannies of economic and social life.

THE SHIFT TO CENTRALISM
Decline set in as the mandarins attempted to do more and more by design.

First officials required farmers to produce in accordance with official decrees, rather than in response to what the market required. Then they insisted on trade with the outside world through quotas.

Possessed of an almost celestial arrogance, the mandarins believed they could micro-engineer all human and social affairs. Cocooned in their remote administrative capital, they issued decrees that encouraged the emergence of corporate monopolies, while regulating ever more aspects of business and commerce. They debauched the currency, making worthless a system of money in pursuit of an imperial design.

I am not, of course, describing Ming China in the fifteenth century, but Europe today.

Europe's agricultural policy means farmers produce what officials decree, not what customers are willing to buy. Quotas govern what textiles and goods Europeans might buy and sell from the world outside. Right across the continent, wealth creators can only produce with official permission.

Starting with coal and steel production sixty years ago, pan-European political institutions have encouraged the creation of a system of monopoly corporatism. So much so that today many of the greatest profits to be gained come not from supplying customers with what they want, but by bidding for government contracts.

Europe's money system – the euro – is not managed in a way that encourages those with capital to invest it in new enterprises. It is run in the interests of governments and bankers who have spent and lent beyond what was wise.

Europe's shift towards centralism started in 1957 with the Treaty of Rome, which established a pan-European political authority for perhaps the first time since the collapse of the Roman imperium in the fourth century. Europe has been steadily centralising ever since. Matters that were once decided by member states are today taken by federal institutions under the doctrine of the *acquis communautaire*.

It is not only Europe that has been centralising. In the United States, the power of the federal government was steadily expanded during the twentieth century. Many of the constraints placed upon federal authority in the Constitution have been set aside.

A series of constitutional amendments in the early twentieth century, followed by the New Deal in the 1930s, meant more power for federal authorities. In the 1950s and 1960s, the federal government expanded its bureaucracy and activity dramatically. States' rights have been gradually eroded – by federal Presidents, Congresses and courts alike.

At the same time, the democratic constraints on those who exercise executive power have been weakened. Successive US Presidents have gained power at the expense of Congress. More and more decisions can be made under presidential fiat and by executive decree.

In Europe, democratic constraints on those who wield executive power at a federal EU level are almost non-existent. The power to initiate new laws rests entirely with a panel of unelected commissioners. The cumbersome, unrepresentative European Parliament is weak and ineffectual at holding the Commission to account. It is more evocative of the supine Spanish Cortes than of the Dutch States-General or the English Parliament.

Far from being a democratic body capable of holding the EU administrative class to account, the European Parliament, elected as it is through the party list system, is a cheerleader for the administrative class. In a return to the pre-modern notion that taxes are for the masses to pay, not the elite, members of the European Parliament do not even have to pay the taxes that their constituents have to pay on pain of imprisonment.[114]

The centralisation of power within the West, and the usurpation of democratic constraints, have removed the kind of systems competition that once helped make the West so innovative. No longer are different European states able to pioneer different approaches to common problems. They are often specifically prevented from doing so. Increasingly, US states have to wait for approval from Washington.

It is not only Washington and Brussels that have centralised power. The growth of supranational institutions and authorities has made it increasingly difficult for different Western states to take different approaches. From immigration policy, to labour law, to international trade, increasingly Western states are left having to comply with directives issued by supranational bodies from on high. Supranationalism makes systems competition impossible, as Western governments are pressurised into adhering to the same bland approaches.

By the end of the twentieth century, on both sides of the Atlantic officials in Washington and Brussels were able to impose precisely the kind of grand, Cartesian designs upon millions of people in a way that would have been unimaginable only a couple of generations ago. By doing so, they have made the West less Western.

DON'T WORRY. THE FUTURE IS BRIGHT

What is the West?

Throughout this book, I have deliberately not defined the term, instead using 'the West' as shorthand for the United States, Canada, Britain, Europe, Japan, Australia and New Zealand. But why this list of nations?

What makes this group of countries 'the West'?

It is not due to geography. Look at a map, and the first thing you notice about these 'Western' nations is that they are not actually on the left-hand side of the chart at all. They are scattered about quite a bit, with Japan, New Zealand and Australia pretty definitely in the east.

Nor is 'the West' some sort of expanded idea of medieval Christendom. There are more church-goers in Nigeria than in Britain today. And more Christians living in South America than in Europe.

Nor even is 'the West' simply Europe writ large. Post-1945 Japan has been very much part of the West. Post-1945 Poland – an integral part of Europe since before the term was invented – was not.

The notion of Westernness is certainly not anything to do with ethnicity or race. Japan's inclusion is proof of that. But so too is the inclusion of the United States – a multi-ethnic nation of immigrants, and perhaps in many ways the Western archetype.

So what is it that makes the West Western?

To see what makes the West Western, we should ask what it is about countries that were once non-Western that changed in order to be regarded as part of the West.

Take Poland or the Czech Republic as examples.

From 1945 to the early 1990s, neither was part of the West. On the contrary, they were – willingly or otherwise – part of a hostile, anti-Western alliance, the Warsaw Pact. Yet today they are as much a part of the West as France, Australia or Canada.

What changed?

You only have to ask to get a sense of how the West is defined by limited government and the existence of internal constraints on power.

It was the constraints placed upon Big Government – not just at Naseby or Yorktown, but at the battles of Legnano and the Downs, too – that helped make the West Western. And perhaps, even more importantly, the restraints imposed by the governed on the governing through Magna Carta at Runnymede and the US Constitution in Philadelphia.

Poland and the Czech Republic joined the West after 1989 not because they changed their flags or signed new treaties. Rather it was because they adopted the notion that the governing had limited power and were accountable to the governed for how they exercised it.

However much the Western elite, in whose interest government grew so big this past century, might imply otherwise, Western civilisation was possible without the state spending more than half the national income. Indeed, it took off precisely because our governing elites were not able to consume the lion's share of wealth the way they did elsewhere.

The West has stalled because our administrative elites increasingly do gobble up what the population produces, demanding that wealth creators seek their permission to produce the wealth that sustains them. Those with a parasitical interest in maintaining the Big Government model will disagree, but it is not cradle-to-grave welfarism that makes the West Western. Neither European social care nor America's Obamacare are what make us part of the civilised world.

It is limited government that defines us as truly Western, for the West did not just flourish when government was small. The West flourished *because* government was limited.

The decision by Poland, the Czech Republic and

other former Communist states to join the West ought to have marked the moment of victory for the Western way of doing things. Our free-market, Hayekian way had prevailed against those in the eastern bloc who sought to organise society in accordance with state socialism.

Alas, it was a pyrrhic victory. The Western way had not prevailed against those inside the West who would still have us arrange our own societies according to other top-down designs.

Since the Berlin Wall came down, the West has retreated yet further away from its model of limited government. In almost every Western state today, the state spends between half and a third as much of GDP as it did when Soviet Communism collapsed. Indeed, in France and Britain today public spending is not far off where it was in certain eastern European states in the last days of Communist rule.

There might have been regime changes within the old Soviet bloc, but within the West, those who believe in moulding society according to their grand designs have become all too firmly entrenched. There has been a seeping current of constructivism running through Western institutions this past generation.

Twenty years after the triumph of the West over Communism, Europe is governed by hardcore Cartesians, as hostile to the free market as they are committed to a grand monetary folly. The West's central banks presume to be able to command the economy much the way central planners run by Marxists once did. Listening to them pontificate about climate change, it seems Western officials believe that they can even make the weather.

Europeanism, environmentalism, Keynesianism, monetarism ... The dogmas invoked to justify intervention in the affairs of men may vary, but the conceit of the interventionists remains the same.

Until now.

The digital revolution will reinvigorate the West, limiting once again the size of government and in the process helping make the West more truly Western. It will enable us to constrain those with power once again.

The digital revolution will do to grand planners in the West what the collapse of Communism did to socialist planners in the old Soviet bloc.

Big Government will become less affordable as the elite find it impossible to keep on concealing the costs of their bloated officialdom. In an increasingly Hayekian world, their Cartesian designs will be rendered ever more redundant. The elite themselves will be displaced in a world where everyone, not just a privileged few, can become a 'secondhand dealer in ideas'. More and more could even become firsthand dealers in ideas, too.

The digital revolution won't simply strengthen many of the old restrictions upon government and officialdom. It will clamp down on new constraints.

Information that once never left the offices of the administrative class will be available to millions. Technology will awaken in millions of people an appetite to decide things for themselves, which will make them increasingly unwilling to abide by decisions foisted on them by remote officialdom.

New networks, founded on reciprocal exchange as much as contractual, will form, creating vast, as yet unimaginable resources of collective intelligence. It will be Google-type systems, rather than government-run systems, that will help guide us through our lives.

Choice and competition, in commerce, ideas and everything, will become the norm.

The West is not doomed. Far from it. Because the future is more Hayekian, our best days lie ahead.

However indebted our Western public finances or sclerotic our economies, such tribulations come from trying to arrange human affairs by constructivist design. They can all be remedied once we quit trying to run the world by top-down design. Fortunately, the digital revolution means we are going to have to.

And that means that in all probability, those who live in what we today call the West will be healthier, wealthier and – yes – happier in several generations' time than those of us living there today.

As Western governments shrink, Western citizens will no longer simply vote in the forlorn hope of getting the public policy priorities that they want. As citizen-consumers they will increasingly set their priorities for themselves, self-commission their children's education and set aside money for their own health accounts.

And as they start to do so, they will find they have far more in common with those millions of middle-class Indians, Brazilians and Chinese who willingly pay for their children's schooling, plan for their old age and set aside money for their families' health care.

In Europe as much as in Asia, the idea of power being vested in unelected and unaccountable mandarins in Brussels or Beijing will become ever more difficult to defend.

The West might not be doomed, but perhaps the

West – or rather Western exceptionalism – is coming to an end.

In the digital age, dispersed power and limited government will no longer be just an imperfectly applied Western ideal in Europe and North America. They will increasingly become a global norm.

Be happy. The West's Big Government model has failed. So we will manage with less government – and rediscover how it was that we once thrived.

NOTES

1   McKinsey Global Institute, *Debt and Deleveraging*, 2012, Charles Roxburgh et al

2   IMF World Economic Outlook database

3   The French government last ran a budget surplus in 1974. Without a significant cut in public spending or rise in taxation, the United States federal government is not projected to run a surplus for the foreseeable future.

4   Calculated as the 'tax wedge' or the difference between workers' take-home pay and the costs of employing them. Data sourced from OECD publication *Taxing Wages* 2011.

5   Estimated percentage of disposable income liable to consumption taxes, such as VAT. Data sourced from Forbes.com article by William P. Barrett 'Average US sales tax rate drops – a little' February 2 2012.

6   'Tax wedge' or the difference between workers' take-home pay and the costs of employing them. Data sourced from OECD publication *Taxing Wages* 2011. VAT rates for UK, France and Germany sourced from Institut Economique Molinari publication *The Tax Burden of Typical Workers in the EU 27* 2011. Data source for Japanese consumption tax from *Financial Times* article March 12 2012, 'Japan seeks to double consumption tax'.

7   Milton Friedman, *Free to Choose*, 1979, p. 37

8   See http://www.usgovernmentspending.com/

9   See http://www.usdebtclock.org/

10 Estimated increase in OECD nation's public debt 2011–2012, divided by 365 days, divided by 24 hours, divided by 60 minutes, then multiplied by 5 minutes.

11 *The Rational Optimist*, Matt Ridley, p. 34

12   Living Costs and Food Survey 2009, pp. 93 and 95
13   Roderick Floud (2011). *The Changing Body – Health, Nutrition and Human Development in the Western World since 1700*, pp. 365–366
14   Research note 102, Taxpayer's Alliance January 30 2012
15   Article by Melissa J. Peterson from *PC World*, September 13 2006
16   *School Workforce in England, November 2011*, Department for Education
17   *After America*, Mark Steyn, p. 208
18   Estimates as to the number of quasi-autonomous non-government agencies vary. In May 2009, the Cabinet Office produced a report claiming there were 766 non-departmental public bodies. In May 2008, the Taxpayers' Alliance estimated that there were 1,148 quangos. Part of the problem is that there is no agreed definition of what constitutes a quango.
19   See http://publications.environment-agency.gov.uk/PDF/GEH O0211BTKV-E-E.pdf
20   *After America*, Mark Steyn, p. 84
21   Cited in *After America*, Mark Steyn, p. 85. Primary source: Clyde Wayne Crews, *Ten Thousand Commandments: An Annual Snapshot of the Federal Regulatory State*, Competitive Enterprise Institute report, June 28 2006.
22   See http://www.civitas.org.uk/pubs/EUFactsheet.php
23   Calculation: $787 billion divided by number of US households, 82.5 million
24   Calculation: £37 billion divided by UK adult population, 36 million
25   For more on the idea that representative institutions in England have their roots in the Anglo-Saxon past, see *The Anglo-Saxon State* by James Campbell.
26   Grover Cleveland had, for example, famously vetoed a trifling $10,000 Bill designed to support farmers on the grounds that there were no grounds for 'such an appropriation in the Constitution'.
27   *Saturn's Children*, Alan Duncan, p. 85
28   *After America*, Mark Steyn, p. 70
29   Table 2:1, *Income Tax Liabilities Statistics*, HM Revenue & Customs, April 28 2011
30   See http://en.wikipedia.org/wiki/Taxation_in_France#Taxes_on_incomes
31   See http://www.financialsensearchive.com/fsu/editorials/dollar daze/2009/0223.html
32   US government spending between 1971 and 2010 rose from less than $1.5 trillion to over $5 trillion at constant 2005 prices.

33 Government spending in Britain between 1971 and 2010 rose from less than £250 billion to over £600 billion at constant 2005 prices. See http://www.ukpublicspending.co.uk/spending_chart_1971_2010UKk_11s1li011mcn_F0t_UK_Public_Spending_As_Per cent_Of_GDP.

34 Centre for Policy Studies paper, *The Hidden Debt Bombshell*, Brooks Newmark, October 19 2009

35 For a more detailed examination of the extent to which media commentators influence political opinion in Britain, see Julia Hobsbawm and John Lloyd's excellent study, 'The Power of the Commentariat', Editorial Intelligence, 2008.

36 See *Guilty Men* by Peter Oborne and Frances Weaver, Centre for Policy Studies, p. 25

37 See *Guilty Men* by Peter Oborne and Frances Weaver, Centre for Policy Studies, p. 26

38 See Robert Peston's *The New Capitalism*, http://www.bbc.co.uk/blogs/thereporters/robertpeston/newcapitalism.pdf

39 See http://www.economist.com/blogs/blighty/2011/09/nature-establishment-opinion

40 See for example, Dan Gardner's excellent book, *Future Babble*.

41 Quoted in *Paper Promises*, Philip Coggan, p. 153

42 British Social Attitudes 28, 2011–2012 edition, NatCen Research, p. 7

43 BBC Politics News, 'Steep drop in public confidence in MPs, says watchdog', September 15 2011

44 'Democracy on Trial', Peter Kellner, YouGov, March 2012

45 European Social Survey data, 2002/03 and 2008/09

46 *The Financial Crisis*, Eamonn Butler, p. 53

47 *Daily Telegraph*, August 2 2011

48 *Evening Standard*, May 31 2011

49 *Evening Standard*, May 31 2011

50 Taxpayers' Alliance report *Wasting Lives*, see http://www.taxpayersalliance.com/wastinglives2011.pdf

51 *Daily Telegraph*, October 13 2011

52 *Mail on Sunday*, January 22 2012

53 Health Service Ombudsman report, February 2011

54 BBC Online, November 9 2011, see http://www.bbc.co.uk/news/health-15639046

55 Care Quality Commission report, see http://www.dailymail.co.uk/health/article-1390925/Elderly-patients-dying-thirst-Doctors-forced-prescribe-drinking-water-old-alive-reveals-devastating-report-hospital-care.html

56 Tullett Prebon report *Thinking the Unthinkable*, p. 45

57 *Sharper Axes, Lower Taxes*, Institute of Economic Affairs, p. 186

58 Tullett Prebon report *Thinking the Unthinkable*, p. 48
59 Social Analysis and Reporting Division, National Statistics Quality Review Series Report number 31 (Office for National Statistics, London, 2004). Quoted in *After America*, Mark Steyn, p. 201
60 *Daily Mail*, September 14 2010
61 See Office of National Statistics data http://www.ons.gov.uk/ons/dcp171776_230487.pdf
62 *Sharper Axes, Lower Taxes*, Institute of Economic Affairs, p. 186
63 Tullett Prebon report *Thinking the Unthinkable*, p. 48
64 *Daily Mail*, August 16 2011
65 *Daily Mail*, August 7 2010
66 *Sharper Axes, Lower Taxes*, Institute of Economic Affairs, p. 172
67 *Sharper Axes, Lower Taxes*, Institute of Economic Affairs, p. 173
68 *Slow Finance*, Gervais Williams, p. 97
69 See *The Coming Fiat Money Cataclysm – and After*, Kevin Dowd et al., November 2011. It suggests that the number of US dollars in circulation has risen from 800 billion to 2.7 trillion, a rise of some 230 per cent since the 2008 crisis began.
70 Raghuram G. Rajan, *Foreign Affairs*, May / June 2012
71 OECD data
72 Tullett Prebon report *Thinking the Unthinkable*, p. 12
73 *The Independent*, November 8 2011
74 *Public Sector Pensions – The UK's Second National Debt*, Neil Record & James MacKenzie Smith, Policy Exchange, 2009
75 *The Coming Fiat Money Cataclysm – and After*, Kevin Dowd et al., November 2011, p. 15
76 *After America*, Mark Steyn, p. 96
77 See www.usdebtclock.org
78 *After America*, Mark Steyn, p. 5
79 Tullett Prebon report *Thinking the Unthinkable*, p. 29
80 Tullett Prebon report *Thinking the Unthinkable*, p. 3
81 Eurostat official statistics
82 *City AM*, 'Eurozone funding eases but fears remain', November 18 2011
83 *Daily Telegraph*, Charles Moore, July 23 2011
84 Ipsos MORI Veracity Index 2011
85 British Social Attitudes survey 28, 2011–12, NatCen Research
86 British Social Attitudes survey 28, 2011–12, NatCen Research
87 British Social Attitudes survey 28, 2011–12, NatCen Research
88 British Social Attitudes survey 28, 2011–12, NatCen Research, p. 7
89 *The Rational Optimist*, Matt Ridley, p. 350
90 See Tyler Cowen's book *The Great Stagnation*, which suggests that increases in productivity as a consequence of computerisation have not been as marked as is often supposed.

91 *The New Road to Serfdom*, Daniel Hannan, p. 54

92 Study by former US Treasury Department economist Martin A. Sullivan

93 *The Guardian*, April 4, 2012

94 *The Rational Optimist*, Matt Ridley, p. 115

95 See the recent 2020 Tax Commission report, which called for a single rate of income tax, amongst other proposals. http://www.2020tax.org/

96 *Paper Promises*, Philip Coggan, p. 32

97 Ludwig von Mises, *Human Action*

98 The 1969 Representation of the People Act removed the 1948 prohibition on political descriptions on ballot papers for parliamentary elections.

99 George Galloway MP, quoted in *Daily Telegraph*, April 21 2012

100 See *The Independent*, December 31 2010

101 *Sunday Telegraph*, March 4 2012

102 Interview with Estonian President Toomas Hendrik Ilves, *T Magazine*, Ernst and Young, Issue 06

103 *The Socialist Case*, Douglas Jay, 1937

104 Perhaps in much the same way that you or I might marvel at the way collective intelligence brings us iPads, our ancestors might have marvelled at the expertise needed to produce sewed leather or iron tools.

105 British Social Attitudes Survey 28, NatCen Research p. 26

106 British Social Attitudes Survey 28, NatCen Research p. 28

107 See British Social Attitudes Survey 28, NatCen Research

108 The West defined as western Europe, North America, Australia, New Zealand and Japan

109 See http://www.economist.com/node/15579727

110 *The West and the Rest in the World Economy*, Angus Maddison, p. 91

111 House of Commons research note. Public debt between 2007 and 2010 increased each year by an average of 4.5 per cent in Japan, 12.8 per cent in the US and 7.3 per cent in the European Union. Source data from IMF and Eurostat.

112 See http://fivethirtyeight.blogs.nytimes.com/2011/08/04/double -dip-or-not-economy-is-falling-farther-behind/

113 *The West and the Rest in the World Economy*, Angus Maddison

114 In a voluntary arrangement introduced by their respective national tax authorities, members of the European Parliament from Sweden and the United Kingdom are billed for income tax in the same way as Swedish and British nationals would be. Members of the legislature from other member states pay no tax on their incomes.

INDEX